T0285326

"Paul Fayad and Chak Fu Lam's *Shaping a Winning Team* is an essential road map for any leader intent on cultivating a top-tier team. This book provides modern and research-backed leadership strategies, giving leaders a strategic approach to not only hire and assess but also to nurture and develop the potential within their teams. It's a testament to the fact that the most successful teams are built through a careful balance of recognizing talent and fostering growth, underpinned by a strong foundation of self-awareness and positive reinforcement. Fayad and Lam have crafted the ultimate guide to shaping a winning culture, no matter the industry or position you're in."

—DR. MARSHALL GOLDSMITH, Thinkers50 #1
Executive Coach and *New York Times* bestselling author of
The Earned Life, *Triggers*, and *What Got You Here Won't Get You There*

"Surrounding yourself with the people you need to succeed is the best decision you can make. *Shaping a Winning Team* helps you do it FASTER, making talent and culture your ultimate competitive advantage."

—PAUL EPSTEIN, former NFL and NBA executive;
bestselling author of *Better Decisions Faster*
and *The Power of Playing Offense*

"The key to a flourishing organization is leadership that is human-centric and compassionate, aware of the power of having the right people all rowing in the same direction. Paul Fayad and Chak Fu Lam illustrate that through their experience, research, and creative approaches to workplace excellence."

—**DEB SMOLENSKY,** global well-being and engagement practice leader and bestselling author of *Brain On!*

"Team cohesion and communication are the lifeblood of a successful organization, and the best mentors know how to develop those skills among their employees. *Shaping a Winning Team*, including the authors' own Positive Assessment Tool, is an accessible journey to help leaders take on this critical task with confidence."

—**BECK BESECKER,** tech entrepreneur and author of *Your Good Work Habits Toolbox*

Shaping a Winning Team

**A Leader's Guide to
Hiring, Assessing, and Developing
the People You Need to Succeed**

Paul Fayad, MSA | Chak Fu Lam, PhD

amplify

an imprint of Amplify Publishing Group

www.amplifypublishinggroup.com

Shaping a Winning Team: A Leader's Guide to Hiring, Assessing, and Developing the People You Need to Succeed

The publisher and the author assume no responsibility for errors, inaccuracies, omissions, or any other inconsistencies herein. All such instances are unintentional and the author's own.

For more information, please contact:
Amplify Publishing, an imprint of Amplify Publishing Group
620 Herndon Parkway, Suite 220
Herndon, VA 20170
info@amplifypublishing.com

Library of Congress Control Number: 2023923985

CPSIA Code: PRV0224A

ISBN-13: 978-1-63755-906-2

Printed in the United States

To "Uncle George"
PF

To my family
CFL

Contents

Foreword

I first met Paul over a decade ago and Chak Fu almost fifteen years ago. I had asked a colleague for a recommendation for a guest speaker who could provide useful information and a unique perspective for my students—someone the students would perceive as both authentic and approachable and, importantly, someone who truly cared about helping students. I was asking for a special kind of speaker indeed. My colleague—and later academic coauthor—Dr. Chak Fu Lam recommended Paul Fayad, with whom he had, by that time, already developed a strong professional and personal relationship that highly influenced many of the ideas you will read in this book.

Since then, I have been honored to maintain a strong relationship with Paul and Chak Fu. Paul continues to speak in nearly every course I teach, from negotiations to leadership to organizational behavior and topics in between. Without fail, he is one of the, if not *the*, most popular speaker each year. Chak Fu and I have continuously worked on research together over the years, and I am constantly impressed by his drive and energy. I'm thrilled they've created this book together.

Paul and Chak Fu's metaphor of rowers, sitters, and drillers is a powerful one. It immediately resonates with people in an almost visceral way, as we all know individuals who fall into each category, including ourselves. My students typically look around the room—sometimes openly, sometimes carefully—as Paul explains the idea, suddenly able to understand their classmates in an enlightened new way. Often there is laughter as everyone realizes they are all looking around similarly. Always there is at least one hesitant hand in the air of someone fearfully wondering if they could possibly be a driller—luckily for them, the fact they wonder this usually implies they are anything but. What Paul and Chak Fu have created in this book is an accessible, well-reasoned, practical guide—replete with stories of Paul's own development—that any leader or employee at any stage can use to self-reflect and improve.

The lessons in this book are science-based and matter-of-fact, but hopeful and taught with a personal flair that makes them especially memorable. I think my students believe both Paul's and Chak Fu's insights because it's clear that with equal passion, they each individually apply them seriously to themselves, even as they encourage others to adopt them. Combined, they're an eclectic and formidable partnership. Paul and Chak Fu make us believe we're in this together; both in the stories in this book and in real life, Paul freely admits the mistakes he's made along the way in his professional and personal development.

We trust this kind of frankness and empathy as we continue our own individual and collective leadership, relational, and development journeys. Overall, this book provides us with a straightforward tool kit of both high-level philosophical insights and down-to-earth, practical behaviors that Paul and Chak Fu have gathered across decades of Paul's own explorations and leadership experience. Paul and Chak Fu's development of a reliable scientific measure of leadership and their clever and useful connections to myriad philosophical and scientific sources help us along this journey.

This book is unequivocally Paul and Chak Fu. It is authentic, it is heartfelt, it is open, and it is wide-ranging but somehow cohesive. It is wise—something I cannot teach my students from within the four walls of a classroom. I always tell my students that Paul reads more widely than almost anyone I know, and Chak Fu is an excellent scholar and teacher. You see this in what Paul and Chak Fu have created here, with threads woven in from philosophy, neuroscience, evolution, social psychology, cognitive science, child development, leadership, culture, religion, and, of course, personal experience.

Yet when the puzzle pieces come together, you realize the profound simplicity and wisdom in the rower-sitter-driller metaphor and all the other vital lessons shared in this book. Paul and Chak Fu have the skill to make you believe what they say. You'll believe this book. And you'll certainly feel inspired to be a rower.

Laura Rees

Assistant Professor of Organizational Behavior
Oregon State University

Preface

If your actions inspire others to dream more, learn more,
do more, and become more, you are a leader.
—John Quincy Adams

Over the last thirty-plus years of running a national health-care services company, providing consulting services on leadership topics, and lecturing at universities in the United States, Canada, and Hong Kong, I became aware of the importance of positive leadership and resulting personality types that would lead to success in the workplace. Developed by using published research on the inheritance of personalities and resulting behaviors and the collection of thousands of assessments, we introduced the concept of R+S+D (rowers, sitters, and drillers) as a crucial part of leadership development at Positive Leader. Based on these inherent personality traits, individuals formed healthier relationships and exhibited extremely successful leadership skills. Over time, we began to see that although not everyone is destined to be a leader, they could use this information for individual improvement and learn to work within their strengths and weaknesses to help build relationships. This book is designed to understand why specific individuals can become successful leaders and workers and how they can be effective through positive leadership. And through positive leadership, it is essential to identify and understand the influence of rowers, sitters, and drillers at work and in their lives. Although the concepts of positive leaders and rowers, sitters, and drillers were initially intended for the workplace, you cannot separate the work environment from the rest of our lives. The overall effort is to become better humans in all our relationships.

The following is a brief introduction to rowers, sitters, and drillers.

Rowers are individuals with a high level of comfort in exhibiting the key personality traits that produce outcomes as leaders or workers. These individuals work hard to develop and maintain solid relationships and are energizers who focus on creating. Tracking the successful leaders and monitoring their results confirmed the assessment data.

On the opposite end of the spectrum, we noticed that individuals who lacked the same personality traits created an atmosphere of negative energy. They drained the significance of the group by complaining, back-channeling, and degrading others. These individuals tend to have egotistical and even narcissistic attributes. They were the opposite of rowers; therefore they were considered drillers.

In the middle of both groups were the sitters. They did not achieve the highest levels of the personality traits determined to produce rowers—nor did they have the lower scores that would designate them as drillers. They were many of the groups willing to sit and follow. At times they may exhibit the traits of the rower, and at times they may demonstrate the traits of the driller.

We have studied the data for the last twenty-five years and realized that although certain personality traits help individuals potentially create stronger relationships, we saw another occurrence. While working with organizations, we were allowed to measure existing staff to determine their ability to form relationships that build strong organizational cultures. This allowed us to work with individuals at different levels of their personalities, communication abilities, and behaviors. This gave us the idea to modify the assessment to include levels of awareness in each trait based on their responses. Instead of just scores and summaries of each trait used to determine their hiring potential, we used levels of awareness: High, Moderate, Minimal, and Monitor. Since the assessment resulted from the individual's responses to critical questions, their awareness was the key indicator of their *comfort* with each personality trait or the resulting behavior of that trait.

The results gave us a new vision of the concept of rower, sitter, and driller with the existing staff. *No* matter their awareness levels, *how individuals use* their traits also determines their ability to form and maintain strong relationships and positive leadership skills.

Rowers are generally empathetic and compassionate. They also get things done, but they do so in motivating and inspirational ways. They care a lot about relationships and can take the perspective of others to recognize what others want and how others feel. In short, they have high levels of emotional intelligence. They are also proactive high achievers who want to go the extra mile to succeed. They thrive in cultures where performance is appropriately rewarded and employees respect one another. These are your star players who tend to speak up with lots of ideas to change and are unafraid of respectfully challenging authority to make things better. They are those in your boat who keep rowing, no matter what. Rowers also accept their levels of awareness, high or low. They do not use their heightened awareness to intimidate others, and they are willing to celebrate the increased awareness of others. They seek to understand their areas of lower awareness, *developing a conscious effort to control and modify their behaviors* to neutralize their undesirable personalities. They are constantly seeking self-improvement while understanding others in the relationship.

Drillers are the opposite of rowers. They are manipulative, driven by self-interest, and tend to be narcissistic. They favor the weak and punish the strong because the strong will threaten their position. They manipulate their interests. They use their high-awareness areas as weapons to control or shame others. If they have low awareness, they attack others who have high awareness to lower the others so they do not have to own up to their behavior. They burn relationships quickly at work and create a toxic culture that leads to employee disengagement. Their relationship focus is selfish, not allowing others to exist. In other words, they drill a hole in your boat—slowly but surely—and sink it in the long run.

Sitters are in the middle. They sit, preferring the status quo, and are not too excited about changes. They become content with their levels of awareness, whether high or low. They desire anonymity, seeking to blend into life without effort. At times they may row if the desire is strong enough, and at times they may drill if persuaded by other drillers. They tend to be content with moving through life by the influence of others, rowing, or drilling. Many individuals are within this level.

When we created the concept of rowers, sitters, and drillers, it was intended for the work environment; however, as we began working with the leaders and staff, we realized rowers rowed in all areas of their life. Therefore, the idea of rowers, sitters, and drillers can apply to our personal lives.

The following pages will provide a breakdown of rowers, sitters, and drillers. We hope you will receive this information as an opportunity to open the window of self-awareness and use these concepts to create a consciousness that leads to healthier decisions, relationships, and life.

How It All Began

Focus on the possibilities for success,
not the potential for failure.
—Napoleon Hill

The *concept* of positive leadership is embraced by many. The *practice* of leading with positivity is challenging, and even those who want nothing more than to be influential leaders may fail in this regard. At its very core, Positive Leader began with a revolt among workers in the 1980s, when I was embarking on my first management assignment—with no formal training. The results could have been disastrous, had it not been for my ability to apply the humbling remediation steps suggested by a mentor to fix what I had inadvertently created through my actions. This experience provided me with the "aha" moment that would drive me to implement positive leadership models in all my future business endeavors.

Here is the story.

The second-shift supervisor of the environmental services department at a local hospital quit. At the time, I was attending college and had been on the job as a full-time employee for six months. The director of the department asked me to assume the shift-supervisor role. Empowered by this new responsibility, I attacked management with a firm hand and stronger words.

I had not yet finished my undergraduate degree. I was years away from my master's degree, focusing on organizational behavior, so my experience managing or leading a staff of thirty-plus people was very limited. Compounding the setup for failure in this situation was the lack of formal orientation to the new role. Still, I was charged with the work production of an entire second-shift environmental services team.

In a matter of weeks, I alienated the entire team with my leadership style, which centered on lecturing them about everything they did wrong. Until days before this promotion, I had been "one of them," so I knew all the tricks they would pull to get out of work and the shortcuts they would take. I told them all that had to stop. I was the boss, and they would have to listen!

That management "technique" failed miserably. Within days, the entire environmental services team had signed a petition, which they took to human resources. The bottom line: they wanted me immediately removed from this management position.

I was devastated. Thankfully, I wasn't fired. But I did have to act. My manager told me I had to meet individually with each person and apologize. First, I had to wrap my head around the fact I was wrong and would be humiliated thirty times over, but the humiliation never came. By fate, the first person I sat down with was Emily, who had worked at the hospital for over twenty years cleaning in the x-ray department. She was an older woman with a contagious smile and a laugh that was deep-bellied and real. In other words, she was very approachable. I sincerely apologized and asked her what she thought would make me a better manager. She said she knew me and supported me as the supervisor because I was kind when working alongside the team. I'll never forget it. She told me, "Don't change who you are, Paul, but learn to trust the ones who can be trusted."

Many of the others I met gave similar responses, though some felt I should leave. I quickly learned I should focus on the team member's strengths. My job was to support them in achieving success. Don't get me wrong—part of that support was to let people go if they chose not to be a part of the team. A year later I was promoted to head of the department, and from there my career as a positive manager took root.

Without the real-world experience of the fear of losing my job and then having to humble myself to my staff, I would not have had that crucial moment that changed the trajectory of my life. It was a critical unveiling that leadership is not about dictating tasks and behavior but about bringing out the best in people and empowering them to succeed.

It is human nature to take certain people and things for granted, and this tendency offers the starting point to understand the dynamics and effectiveness of the Positive Leader methodology.

According to my coauthor, Dr. Chak Fu Lam, who has a PhD in management and organization, "High-energy, productive staff members—whether leaders or employees—are often left to conduct their work in a vacuum of feedback. This is largely because they can be counted on to continue at their high level of productivity and innovation. Eventually, however, without positive recognition or constructive evaluation, these highly skilled, high-producing employees will leave."

The key is to understand each person better and identify which hiring candidates or current employees have the personality to be a positive energizer who can contribute to the organization's overall success. As science suggests, it is vital to remember that personality is essentially unchangeable. A complex organization of traits determines how a person will act, think, and feel. Personalities reflect who a person is at their core. While the person may wish to be different, research has proven that overall personality change is challenging and takes a long time. The degree of potential change is minimal.

That promotion to shift supervisor at a local hospital was the start of my journey down the path of positive leadership. I was in my early twenties and was simultaneously pursuing an undergraduate degree in a premed program. That first experience in management and realizing the cost of a medical degree changed my trajectory from medicine to attending business school. I successfully earned a bachelor of science in small business management and entrepreneurship. Eventually, as I moved through the ranks of upper management, I completed my graduate degree in business administration, with a focus on organizational behavior. The ability to work in the field of my education was priceless. I began to recognize the unquestionable impact of rewarding employees with high levels of positive energy—those who were focusing on their work and experiencing success—versus trying to fix those who instead chose to work against leadership and create logjams.

Ultimately, as I worked my way to higher levels of management, I was hired by a privately owned health-care management services organization, HHA Services. I was promoted to higher responsibilities through positive leadership techniques, eventually becoming the president and CEO. Along the way, HHA won many customer and employee satisfaction awards, becoming a model for others in the industry because of its high service quality and employee retention. The best managers at HHA led positively—not just through affirming words but by infusing the work ecosystem with their energy. When these encouraging managers provided constructive conversations with staff members to correct certain behaviors, they focused on what needed to be accomplished, not what they had done wrong. They also provided examples of successful outcomes in other areas of the organization. This style of positive leadership creates a learning process for the employee.

Chak Fu was working on his PhD in organizational behavior at the University of Michigan when we met through my son, Andrew, a research assistant to Chak Fu. Chak Fu approached the Positive Leader philosophy from a different but essential angle—academics and science. He provided the research and analytics that fully supported the Positive Leader contention that human beings respond more favorably to positive comments and leadership than to negative or passive-aggressive remarks and reviews.

The two roads converged on the path to creating Positive Leader, LLC. As such, we teamed up to undergo this personnel journey from a holistic perspective, linking practical business experiences with science and academics. The result is a model that focuses first on the personalities of organizational members and then on the skill levels they bring and those that can be improved while constantly infusing positive feedback to achieve the desired results.

The creation of Positive Leader began as a program under HHA Services, and I developed a program that would orient new personnel to the concepts of positive leadership. The delivery model at the time was called Q-School, with the Q standing for *Quality*. It was a two-day training program for supervisory management and executive hires to learn about Total Quality Management and how to create an engaged workforce. The training was thoroughly vetted to be accessible to anyone, yet the results were inexplicably inconsistent and varied.

Even though the Q-School participants were given the same information, delivered in the same way, and with the same supporting materials, the results were neither predictable nor sufficiently successful. I was baffled why the curriculum—administered to all participants similarly—did not produce consistent results. I was very engaged in determining what was occurring during the instruction phase and afterward in applying this new, positive method of leadership. Taking a step back made it clear why this wasn't a concept or training that would produce the same results 100 percent of the time.

We realized that although everyone attended and passed the two days of instruction, subsequently, when we measured the results at each location, they seemed randomly unpredictable. But after closer observation and evaluation, the reason became apparent. It appeared the individuals we trained had what we eventually determined to be personality traits that ultimately filtered into their behavior. We saw that the managers who embraced the program and were able to create positive environments on the job were highly successful.

We objectively measured success through third-party surveys of team members, clients, and customers at each location. Effective managers took on more responsibilities and were more likely to be successful in their positions. Additionally, we noticed that they continued to exhibit positive leadership traits when they advanced to new positions. The results indicated that they were generally considered positive people who could embrace and apply the teachings of positive leadership and apply them.

This should not be construed as a Pollyannaish vision that being positive will solve all organizational issues. Instead, it is a starting point that can be used to create solid teams and relationship-based culture. Sometimes it will be necessary to make tough decisions regarding staff members who cannot meet the department or organization's needs. Managers with high levels of empathy, compassion, and emotional intelligence are assumed to struggle with making these hard decisions. The result is that they will continue to allow issues to fester, believing they can modify certain staff members' bad behavior and save the individual. Drillers are where leaders can go wrong. Because they may be highly skilled workers, leaders may ignore that they are drillers, and they will destroy the organization's culture. Leaders will then spend more time focusing on trying to change the driller's mindset.

Rowers create an energized atmosphere. They make managing and leading easy because they focus on producing positive outcomes. We see them as champions leading the team without much need for supervision. Managers make the mistake of ignoring them, which can cause frustration to the rowers, and ultimately they will leave. Sitters need goals established and need to be managed throughout the process. For them, it may just be a job, an opportunity to make a living, and this needs to be understood by the manager.

Throughout this book, we will see the relationship between positive leadership principles; the utilization of an assessment to measure specific personalities and the resulting behaviors; and the concept of rowers, sitters, and drillers as the overall result of establishing what we would call a "positive ecosystem."

The manager's job is understanding each team member's personality and behavior. The following chapters will clarify how to achieve this goal and, through positive leadership, improve productivity and decrease turnover. It will also introduce the responsibility of leaders to not only be the best leader in relationship to the work environment but to be representative of the best a human can be. Great leaders tend to row in all areas of their lives.

PART I

Rowers, Sitters, and Drillers

CHAPTER 1

The Origin of Rowers, Sitters, and Drillers

Being the best you can be is a demand.
Failing that demand is the betrayal of you.
—Dhyan Vimal

During a late dinner and discussion, with many notes taken and diagrams depicted on paper, Chak Fu and I were preparing for an upcoming leadership presentation at a hospital in northern Michigan. The presentation included a section on personalities and skills. As we discussed this presentation aspect, the concern was what would be included and how it would be delivered. We knew there had to be a better way to explain the differences and, more importantly, to illustrate the impact that personalities have on an organization's ability to flourish or struggle and how behaviors—or skill sets—have fewer permanent implications because they can be modified and improved.

We reviewed the collected data and understood which personality traits successful managers exhibited and which were lacking in unsuccessful managers; unsurprisingly, they were usually the same. The problem was providing a visual presentation allowing attendees to thoroughly comprehend how the different personalities affected the staff. We understood that imagery and visualization are vital to the learning process.

With that knowledge, the image of a rowboat and the idea of rowers, sitters, and drillers came to life. A boat was certainly something anyone could picture in their mind. And while boats are generally stable, they are typically best and serve their purpose when maintaining forward motion and not taking on water.

We knew the analogy of a boat representing a business was perfect. The boat's desire to reach a chosen destination most effectively and efficiently created the need for the best team to provide the energy. The birth of rowers, sitters, and drillers fulfilled the necessity of distinguishing which individuals would influence the movement and produce the correct energy—or destroy the momentum.

Rowers, Sitters, and Drillers in the Workplace

While the world may need all kinds of people, businesses don't. That may sound harsh, but it is true when discussing personalities. Based on research and practical application, the Positive Leader team learned that certain personalities could provide the talent needed for managers and leaders to become strong relationship builders within organizations. Rowers are highly motivated employees who take pride in getting the job done. They row! While doing this, they also bring positive energy that translates into getting along with others and inspiring them. Sitters tend only to do what is minimally expected of them and can be swayed to take on traits of a rower or driller, whichever is more dominant. Drillers are negative-energy people who find faults in how things are done, managed, and processed. While they may have exceptional skills on paper, they don't always employ them in their work, choosing instead to grumble and cause moderate to serious disruption in the workplace. While others are rowing, or at least not hindering progress, the drillers are in the back of the boat, drilling a hole in the bottom to sink it.

Generally speaking, most organizations are fortunate if they have some rowers, and the reality is they primarily employ sitters and sadly allow drillers to stay on their teams. Why would any organization allow someone as destructive as a driller to remain? And why would they tolerate the uninspired work of sitters?

Rowers

This is a small but influential group in many organizations. These people are energizers, focused and self-directed individuals who are naturally positive, and it is who they are at their core. Rowers have a great attitude, and they constantly want to excel at their jobs.

Within an organization, rowers are individuals who are empathetic and compassionate. They not only get things done but also do so in ways that are motivating and inspirational to others.

They care deeply about relationships and can step into the perspective of others to know what they want and how they feel. They have high emotional intelligence, self-awareness, and the capacity to be aware of others' feelings. They are highly proactive achievers who will take the initiative to see a project through, even if it means more work. They are also agreeable, which is directly linked to their ability to have and express compassion and empathy. They can put others' needs before their own and often do. Their goal is for the organization or the project to succeed, and they will do what is necessary to make that happen.

Rowers characteristically thrive in cultures where their performance is appropriately rewarded and employees respect one another. Rowers are your conscientious star players who are not afraid to speak up with ideas to change how things are done for the betterment of all. They are also not afraid to challenge authority if they believe it will improve the work environment or end products. All this said, rowers will also listen to subject-matter experts and will engage in spirited dialogue to better understand the reasoning behind decisions. They are those in your boat who will keep on rowing no matter what.

A great benefit of having rowers on your team is that they see themselves for who they are. This self-awareness helps them see others for who they are, which often translates into getting along with everyone—except drillers.

Sitters

Forming much of the workforce, these employees are happy with their production and relationships. They are not always energized but can rise to the occasion when needed.

THE ORIGIN OF ROWERS, SITTERS, AND DRILLERS

This group comprises the bulk of your leadership and employee base. They are also the most unremarkable. Sitters are neither too empathetic nor too manipulative. They sit. And wait. They don't rock the boat. Sometimes you wonder if they know they're in the boat. Sitters prefer the status quo and neither show strong support nor oppose changes.

Most importantly, sitters look at what others do. If others are rowing, they row a little. If others are drilling, they drill a little. They are your average worker who does just enough to get things done and keep their job. They rarely exceed your expectations and never lead their group to higher ground. They are not the people to turn to for ideas on changing processes for greater efficiencies or better outcomes. In other words, they simply go with the flow. They don't row the boat hard but don't drill holes. Because the majority of the workforce belongs to this category, there is no doubt why organizations fail to maintain inspired forward momentum.

Drillers

In the review of drillers, it is best to say they are the opposite of rowers since they do not possess the same levels of compassion and empathy and rarely lead to change. At best, they are egotistical and self-centered. The higher-level drillers tend to be narcissists, focusing on how everything around them affects their world and manipulating the people and environment around them to their advantage. When managers fail to take actions to address these drillers and focus their full attention on these drillers, the drillers thrive. This is because drillers often mistake attention for an acknowledgment of their importance. Focus on them, and they ensure you know just how important they are.

They strive to be influential and can become informal leaders of organizations; this status is generally gained through intimidation or gaslighting. They will react if pressured, but not in a positive way.

Drillers, whether managers or employees, are manipulative and driven by self-motivation. They favor those who follow them and are antagonistic toward the strong because the latter is seen as threatening to their position. Drillers manipulate situations and others to advance their interests.

Moreover, drillers are masters at playing the game. In front of management, they can appear submissive and nonthreatening. But when management is not around, they act entirely out of self-interest. They may seem like a friend to you, but once they do not see you as beneficial to them, they may ignore you or place blame in your direction. This can include blackmailing or talking negatively about you to those who matter—or those who will spread this gossip. They burn relationships quickly, and in the long run, they create a toxic culture that leads to complete employee disengagement. In other words, they drill a hole in your boat—slowly but surely—and keep it from moving forward. In dealing with the impact of drillers, managers are in constant reaction mode, fixing the holes. This leaves little time for much else. This may seem like an extreme definition of drillers. It is essential to understand that although they comprise a small group of workers in most cases, their influence can disrupt the positive culture of organizations.

Our company was given the opportunity to work with a medical center in Chicago. While implementing our program, we would meet with the department's staff on each shift. This allowed us to get to know the team and provide them with transparency and an opportunity for their input regarding potential changes to their work schedules, processes, and equipment. During the meetings, the staff was very engaged. They offered support and ideas and provided insight as to why the current methods were in place. Over the next few months, as we implemented the changes, we began to see the effects of the rowers leading the changes and providing solid feedback. They were engaged and committed to seeing improvements. The drillers started complaining about the changes, not offering alternatives but insisting the initial processes were better. Their complaints were not to our management team but the staff attacking those supporting the change during breaks. They started a campaign to complain to other departments, spreading disinformation. They even came to our managers one-on-one and blamed others for the disinformation. Their behavior would have been tolerated in most cases because they had seniority and were highly skilled at work. The reality was, production—and the overall quality—was suffering.

In most cases, the result would have been to return to the old processes. But our leadership team was well trained in dealing with drillers. Through proper communications with personnel and the facilities administration, as well as isolating specific behaviors that would lead to following a correct termination format for the drillers, they could remove them from the department. The result was immediate improvements in productivity and quality. This process took more than one year to complete, and during this period the individuals were given many opportunities to improve. The lost opportunity during this time was all the focus was on the drillers, and the managers had to remember that others were producing excellent outcomes. This is where recognition is essential to maintaining engagement and positivity.

Presenting R, S, and D Data

Looping back to the dinner conversation between Chak Fu and myself, we knew we needed to add another aspect to the rowers, sitters, and drillers model. While the image of the boat and the three types of people in it was a helpful visual, we needed a graphic or chart representation that could show how everyone presents themselves. This grid representation also required to exhibit how skills—both of which can be modified—impact the performance of rowers, sitters, and drillers.

The result was a three-by-three matrix. This provides an accurate image of the interaction of personalities and behaviors—which, in this case, will be referred to as skill sets—in hiring, managing, and establishing positive relationships. The top-three areas of the matrix identifiers became rowers, sitters, and drillers (matrix 1).

Matrix 1

	Rowers	Sitters	Drillers

Behaviors and Skill Sets

Along the left side of the matrix 2 individuals' skill sets, A represents the highest skill set. B is the next highest skill set, and C identifies the lowest. Using a sports analogy, think of the A players as those in the starting lineup. They have the highest skill levels. The B players have the next highest skill level and are the replacements when the A players need a rest; they come off the bench. The C players are rookies or minor-league players. They have the lowest skill levels but show potential. Remember: skills can be learned or modified through training and proper direction; therefore C players can become B and even A players. Likewise, B players can become A players.

Matrix 2

	Rowers	Sitters	Drillers
A			
B			
C			

The Eighty-Twenty Rule

It is human nature to focus on what is wrong while ignoring what is right. This goes back to the beginning of humankind when the bulk of the day was spent trying to avoid death at the hands of a predator or the elements. Therefore, most of the time was spent maintaining shelter, staying warm, finding food, and resting. It might have been noticed if something was going right, but little time would be spent practicing gratitude. Survival, not reveling in good fortune, was the mission.

Even though we are far from those times, instincts still rule. Of course, we are not trying to survive in the workplace physically. Fear was the motivator for our ancient ancestors and shouldn't be ours. Instead, the workplace must be a place for exploration of opportunity and excitement over the ability to provide our service or product to our community and our world. To make that happen, we cannot be led by fear. Instead, we must be guided by possibility. This is the foundation of Positive Leader and why so many companies have been able to chart a successful and more harmonious course by using these tools and principles.

This is a philosophical shift that innately positive leaders will enthusiastically embrace. Those who are not positive tend to resist it—not just because they lack the belief that leading with positivity will work but because it is nearly impossible for them to do so. Again, it is not in their DNA. They will hold on to the old way of leading by intimidation and fear, with a focus on the negative and what is not working. They will more than likely think that leading with positivity is a Pollyanna business model.

That is a shortsighted and foolish belief.

Typically, most managers and leaders—whether they are positive people or not—place 80 percent of their focus on 20 percent of their staff, bowing to the instinct of concentrating on what is wrong. It's like seeing a fire and instinctively wanting to put it out. Unfortunately, this means they are focusing the overwhelming majority of their attention on the drillers in hopes of turning them into sitters or even rowers. Their objective is to improve the work of the drillers.

But as we learned earlier in this chapter, drillers do not change. They will always complain, and their personality tendency is to be negative. They will always act selfishly and resist change not initiated by them. Moreover, they are perfectly comfortable being this way.

The mere act of focusing on the drillers does not translate to improving workplace quality or increasing production. Not only does it not change the drillers but sitters, through the concept of social learning, will most assuredly take on the actions of the drillers because the drillers are getting attention. This dynamic—called social learning—is explored in many studies. The most significant takeaway, however, is that focusing on the problem tends to compound it by encouraging others to talk about problems and issues rather than opportunities and possibilities. This results in a further lowering of productivity and the quality of work.

Matrix 3 represents where leaders spend eighty percent of their focus on twenty percent of their team. Keep in mind that those in the *A-line* have top skill sets, followed by *B* and then *C*, which reflects diminishing skill sets. Regardless of their skill set, drillers are detrimental to culture and overall productivity, and drillers cannot change. Sitters or rowers with *C*-level skill sets present room for improvement.

Most managers believe they can change the behavior of the damaging drillers, so they focus on trying to do just that. But by focusing on the unchangeable drillers, they largely ignore those doing a great job (rowers) or a reasonably good job (sitters). So not only does practicing this misguided approach affect no change in the drillers but the leader is also, in essence, punishing the productive employees with zero attention and feedback.

As seen with social learning, sitters who witness the attention given to the drillers become drillers themselves and begin drilling. Why? They want attention. The result: productivity and quality both suffer. Equally as bad, rowers become frustrated and will leave the organization. Of course, during the process of focusing on the drillers, with attempts to instruct change, you may be able to terminate them over time. But your culture and work output have suffered by then, possibly beyond repair.

Matrix 3

	Rowers	Sitters	Drillers
A			Heavy Focus
B			Heavy Focus
C	Focus	Focus	Heavy Focus

The Positive Leader Focus

The basic premise of positive leadership is that people react favorably to positive feedback. Research has shown that when someone smiles at a person, that person tends to smile back. Along the same line, the first reaction when someone punches you is likely to punch them back.

Positive leaders approach rowers with a smile, which rewards exemplary work and recognizes their self-directed behavior as presenting a positive presence. They provide positive feedback to those who contribute the most to the company. As a result, these leaders see success in processes that produce excellent results and can mirror the results in other areas of the organization.

Matrix 4 illustrates a scenario in which attention is given mainly to employees who are rowers and sitters at all skill levels. This is done because of their ability and willingness to learn, and Rowers and sitters can grow their skill sets.

When positive leadership is exercised, rowers row harder, and sitters can slowly behave like rowers (social learning). Additionally, C players can improve faster and become B or A players. It is given that rowers will happily learn ways to become A performers because they *want* to be A performers. As a result, productivity and quality increases. Not only that but you have completely shifted the dynamic and energy of your workforce. The positive personalities will now have a chance to infuse their essence into the rest of the team. It's almost like hitting cruise control or autopilot. The force of positivity will begin to take over. Miraculously, sitters will start seeing the respect given to the rowers and want to be more like them. The entire culture and direction of your workforce will effectively change.

Matrix 4

	Rowers	Sitters	Drillers
A	Focus	Focus	
B	Focus	Focus	
C	Focus	Focus	

As you can see in Matrix 4, the drillers receive minimal attention when focusing primarily on rowers and sitters. This is like cutting off their life support. Drillers cannot exist without attention. There will be a time when they will drill harder to gain the attention they so desperately need, especially at the beginning, when you start ignoring them. But without this attention, they will, thankfully, eventually leave the organization, or through proper documentation, they will be terminated.

The Difficult Decision

Each organization has specific processes for dealing with critical conversations and, ultimately, the termination of individuals within their organization. Following such processes consistently and without emotion is vital in removing drillers from your organization. The difficulty presents itself when managers with high levels of compassion and empathy have difficulty in the termination process. Their first effort is to save the individual, thinking they can change them. As stated above, delaying the process creates more uncertainty within the organization. In advising managers on deciding to terminate drillers in their organization, I refer to the famous words of Mr. Spock from *Star Trek II*: "The needs of the many outweigh the needs of the few." Positive leaders who hope to salvage everyone need to remind themselves that the others within the organization should be the ones who are protected from the adverse effects of drillers. As leaders, it is our responsibility to be protectors. Positive leaders accept this responsibility.

What If My Highly Skilled Team Member Is a Driller?

A common and understandable mistake many managers make is that they are unwilling to let go of drillers who are A performers.

They try to reprimand them and correct their negative behavior, but this will not stick, because it is the personality that needs to change. This cannot happen. As a note, drillers survive in the workplace because they have learned how to navigate to get their way. Compounding the damage of this situation is that by holding on to that one "top" performer, managers may turn sitters into drillers, creating a more significant workforce problem. Even more significantly, they will most assuredly disenfranchise their rowers, who positively impact the company.

In trying to save one high performer who is negative, you are sacrificing many of your most reliable and best performers. To preserve their organization, it is imperative that leaders place their primary focus on the rowers and take action to eliminate the drillers.

Management professor Dr. Sandra Robinson from the University of British Columbia observed patterns of social learning during work situations. She found that sitters were likelier to demonstrate negative behaviors when they witnessed drillers acting negatively. On the other hand, rowers won't engage in negative behaviors, but they will grow increasingly dissatisfied with a team of drillers. Eventually, the rowers will leave the organization.

Conversely, when you focus on rowers, you signal to the rest of the team that positivity is rewarded. Once the sitters see you focusing your time and energy on the rowers, they will mimic the rowers' behaviors and become more positive. This is how a positive culture takes shape, creating a holistic ecosystem rooted in positivity and reward.

Exceptions to the Rowers, Sitters, and Drillers Categorization

At this time, it is essential to point out that while individuals with certain inherent personality traits usually fit cleanly into one of the three boat categories, there are circumstances when, for instance, a sitter temporarily becomes a driller, or a rower becomes a sitter or even a driller.

These temporary shifts can happen due to extraordinary life circumstances, such as a death in the family, a divorce, trouble with children, upsetting financial situations, etc. But leaders who genuinely know their employees will identify whether this is an anomaly or if they have read the person wrong. Having a conversation with the employee can help reveal any underlying issues and allow the leader to help support the employee through the troubling time in their lives and return to their true self.

In her book *The How of Happiness*, Sonja Lyubomirsky, PhD, explains how to manage the slings and arrows life throws at us. Her chapter on managing stress, hardship, and trauma provides readers with coping strategies. She explains that over time we can thrive after we have met our challenges, using different coping methods during recovery.

Similarly, the study *Adapting to life's slings and arrows: Individual differences in resilience when recovering from an anticipated threat* by Christian E. Waugh, Barbara L. Fredrickson, and Stephan F. Taylor addresses who is best equipped to recover from trauma. Not surprisingly, the main finding from this study was that high-trait, resilient participants showed complete affective recovery when presented with a neutral picture after anticipating a possible aversive picture. Resilience, albeit a behavior that can be learned, was positively correlated with two personality traits: optimism and emotional stability.

Finding a Balance as a Rower

I opted to lead through intimidation and force when I was first allowed to lead at a very young age. It backfired magnificently, and from that, I was able to choose between growth as a person or trying again to muscle through the changes I thought at the time were correct. Instead, I embraced the learning experience and overcame my pride to adjust to a positive management style.

Based on only hiring candidates with certain positive inherent personality traits, my company, HHA Services, achieved remarkable success. The company won the coolest places to work in southeastern Michigan over multiple years from 2010 to 2013; it was also rated in the top twenty-five "Best Places to Work in Healthcare" by *Modern Healthcare Magazine* in 2010 and 2011. Additionally, in 2004, HHA was awarded the Lighthouse Award by the Michigan Quality Council as measured by the prestigious national Baldrige organization.

On an operational level, after implementing the Positive Leader assessments and practices, turnover at HHA fell from more than 30 percent to a single digit, and business boomed as it became one of the largest privately owned support services companies in the United States.

This story is important because it illustrates that even rowers will immediately fall into the trap of instinctually approaching a situation with force and intimidation. This should encourage leaders who have traveled a similar negative-response road.

A Positive Leader Success Story

At one point in my work at a health-care services company, we signed a new agreement with a large medical center in southeast Michigan. Our company was to be responsible for the environmental services department, which included more than three hundred employees working seven days a week, twenty-four hours per day. When we took over the department, morale was low, performance suffered, and turnover was high. In addition, the health-care provider's third-party surveys of the staff and patients were some of the lowest scores in the region. The multiyear contract would only be renewed if we could turn around the survey scores and provide positive performance results in all areas.

Our Positive Leader team went to work. Phase one was multiple meetings on all shifts with all staff members. Critical questions asked were:

- What are we doing right?
- What must we do to ensure the proper work is accomplished?

The staff pointed out successful areas. These were typically areas where they had previously worked and built on established relationships with the clinical staff. An example would be communicating with nurses about their preferences regarding the work of the health-care services representatives.

As the conversations and analyses progressed within the health-care services team, we noticed the most relevant issues hindering improved performance, including proper equipment, recognition, celebrations for good performance, and enhanced relationships between staff and management of the department and with other medical center personnel.

The turnaround began when we highlighted, celebrated, and mirrored successes in other areas. Equipment was updated, which helped the staff perform at a higher and more efficient level. The staff saw management helping and playing a part in their day-to-day activities.

As a result of these action steps, positive relationships grew with the medical center staff, and the team gained self-confidence. Most importantly, the staff who deserved recognition received it daily. Not surprisingly, the rowers rowed harder, many of the sitters started rowing a bit more, and the drillers, over time, were terminated or left.

Within the first year, the third-party survey results climbed from the lowest tier in the state to the highest. Notably, this was a unionized staff, so members had recourse if they felt what was being implemented either added to their responsibilities or was in any way unfair. The key to adoption and adaptation was constant communication, focusing on success and not failure.

The above example is one of many successful outcomes we have experienced throughout the company. When embraced, the concept of rowers, sitters, and drillers provided a strong blueprint for leaders to become positive leaders. The results were conclusive. When we focus our attention on the positive outcomes of the rowers, acknowledging their success, they row harder. Sitters, through social learning, want acknowledgment, so they begin to row. Production and quality improve. And drillers will stand out for the lack of cooperation.

CHAPTER 2

The Tao of the Rower

Knowing others is intelligence; knowing yourself is true wisdom. Mastering others is strength; mastering yourself is true power.

—Lao Tzu

A master was planning a trip up a long and treacherous river to pay respects to *his* master, who had long passed. This master selected three students to be a part of his journey. The first student was a high-energy, compassionate, and well-learned student who had been with the master for only a short period of time. The second student had been with the master for many years and was quite comfortable, having recently achieved a higher rank. The third student had been with the master for a few years and was known as a difficult student.

The master and the three students jumped into the boat,

which was large enough to have a quiet area the master could use to meditate in private. All three students began rowing the boat. After a while, the third student stopped rowing and started complaining about the master meditating while they rowed.

"Why doesn't Master row? This is so unfair," the third student lamented.

After a while, the second student, noticing that the third student had stopped rowing and feeling that he had the most seniority, also stopped rowing and sat peacefully, staring at the clouds in the sky. The first student, seemingly unaffected by the decisions of the other two students, quietly started rowing harder. When the master completed his meditation, he made enough noise so the second and third students could resume rowing to avoid getting into trouble.

The first student silently rowed.

The third student complained to the master privately that the second student had not kept up with his rowing responsibilities while the master was meditating. The master listened but took no immediate action. When they were a few hours from the village, the master thanked the first student for his continuous effort. He praised the student and sat beside the first student to learn more about his goals.

Noticing this, the second student started picking up the pace, and eventually, the master praised the second student's effort.

Unaffected by the trend on the boat, the third student continued to complain about the others and the pace, which had increased twofold because the other students were working in harmony. But those complaints fell on deaf ears. The master was focused on the excellent work of the first two students and knew they would get to the village in record time. The master was grateful and filled with bliss.

When the group reached the village, the master asked the third student to moor the boat and get fresh water for the trip home. He then took the first two students to the temple where his master was buried. As a reward, he allowed the two students to enter and celebrate with him.

On the way back to the boat, the master stopped and spoke to a friend who made a living fishing. The friend told the master he needed help on his boat and asked if he could spare a student for a year. If so, he would send fish to the master's village.

"The work is hard, but the rewards are many," said the friend. The master looked at the two students who made the trip into town with him and offered the friend to take his first student. When he sat with the first student to let him know, the student was upset, and the master allowed him to speak freely. The student asked, "Why would you let me go when I was the best rower on the boat, and I don't know how to fish?"

The master smiled and replied, "Because you are the best and do not need me to help you be the best anymore. This is my friend, and I trust you will serve him well."

The student then asked the master why he brought the third student if he knew he was a complainer. The master replied, "Because I wanted to make sure the student could not change by giving him another chance. I also wanted to see if my second student would be able to be a rower and not a sitter."

The first student bowed to the master and set off to work for the master's friend. On the way home, the master focused his attention on the second student, who continued to row hard even though the first student was no longer there to inspire him. The third student continued to complain, now focusing on the fact there were only two students left to row. When they were close to the master's village, the master threw the third student overboard.

In the business world, we see this play out often. Our rowers work hard, focusing on providing exceptional outcomes. Yet they work alongside sitters who will do the minimal, viewing their results as needed to maintain their employment. Drillers create an atmosphere of chaos, destroying the culture. Leaders need to recognize the signs of disruption the drillers cause before losing their rowers.

The point is, rowers row, sitters sit, and drillers drill. Personalities are highly unlikely to change, and this means drillers will not stop drilling, just as rowers will not stop rowing. This also means you need to find rowers. To do this, you must know what personality traits make up a rower.

Let's look at what rowers have in common regarding personalities.

High on the list of personality traits are openness, emotional stability, empathy, and conscientiousness. Simply put, rowers have a high degree of seeing the other person or a situation with an open mind. They are people who can care enough to understand the needs of another or what is needed in a particular case without prejudice. This is also referred to as cognitive empathy. Yet they are also deliberate in their compassion, knowing when and how much to help.

Rowers form a supportive, creative environment by exhibiting high levels of gratitude and praise. They understand the concept of teamwork and strive to create a cooperative environment.

Notably, rowers also have high energy and will be the ones who jump into situations when others hesitate. Energy *must* be considered when we refer to rowers. Their ability to rise to all occasions and be present always requires energy. In addition to rowers exhibiting high levels of emotional intelligence and empathy, rowers also bring forth high levels of relational energy.

In 2015 Bradley Owens, Wayne Baker, Dana McDaniel Sumpter, and Kim Cameron brought forth the term *relational energy* to denote the positively or negatively charged interactions within the work environment that exert measurable effects on workplace performance and personnel, as well as business success. Previous research by Baker, Rob Cross, and Wooten (2003) confirmed that, within an organization, others' positive energy could improve our job performance and knowledge acquisition.

In another study by Quinn, Spreitzer, and Lam (2012), energy is an organizational resource that increases employees' capacity for action and motivation, enabling them to do their work and attain their goals.

Simply put, we want to be around energetic coworkers who are kind and compassionate. They make us want to row!

Our health-care services company decided to start a food services division. Since the company had minimal experience in institutional food services, our team needed to find a division manager who could create a solid team and hit the ground running. We needed a highly skilled rower.

We had met such a person and knew this person had just left a competitor company. During the hiring process, our company used a personality assessment tool to ensure this individual met the criteria based on personality. They needed to identify and match the correct personality that would help to establish and grow the department quickly.

Fortunately, our desired candidate passed the assessment and was willing to create a new service line for our company. Over the next decade, we built a strong food services division throughout the United States. This new vice president overseeing the new area had proven his ability, but most importantly, he was respected by all those who worked for him, and his team excelled in all areas.

Each year during the employee questionnaire process, his division and team scored the highest in the company. He was a compassionate and conscientious leader. And although he knew more about the business than everyone, he was always willing to listen and adapt to new ideas.

It is important to note that true leadership is not so much about leading others to follow but leading as an example for others to respect and see what could be if they were to lead.

Rowers row not to claim victory; they row to set an example. They row because they are genuinely grateful to row. In a spiritual sense, they see their rowing as a blessing, an honor, not a task associated with their ego. The personality traits of hundreds, if not thousands, of rowers we have worked with have all been linked to high levels of openness, emotional intelligence, empathy, conscientiousness, adaptability, and an intrinsic desire to learn. In the end, they are the ones who show up and produce with a joyful heart.

When Rowers Stop Rowing

A question that often arises is whether rowers can become sitters or even drillers. The answer is yes, and no. Rowers can stop rowing if they feel their work is not appreciated, the organization's integrity is questioned, or the direct manager is not following the mission or the intent of positive leadership.

Our management experience has shown that rowers will continue to row but will voice their complaints to management or their team leaders. They can become vocal and appear to be drillers, but the difference is they are not trying to sink the boat; instead, they are doing their best to keep it afloat based on what they know and what they think is correct. They will often provide constructive criticism combined with potential solutions. In management research, voice behavior is a type of upward communication of ideas, suggestions, or concerns intended to benefit the unit or the organization. Chak Fu has spent more than a decade studying this phenomenon, and studies have consistently shown that such voice behavior, if listened to, enhances unit and team performance. The bottom line is that rowers sometimes become sitters, wholly frustrated and ambivalent about the organization's direction. This generally leads to their departure from the organization, as they see their effectiveness limited or negated due to management issues. Successful managers recognize this is happening before it is too late.

How Do We Get Sitters to Row?

This is also a common question; the answer is simple and complex. When discussing positive leadership, you must focus attention on your rowers; then, through social learning, sitters will begin rowing a bit more. Of course, sitters can always row; they just lack the inspiration to do so. The experience of Positive Leaders is that when provided with consistent feedback on their successes and a focus on their development, sitters can become rowers. Therefore, sitters need constant reinforcement that it is appreciated when their work is excellent.

Drillers Drill!

Finally, many ask: Can drillers become sitters or even rowers? The answer lies in the genetic composition of drillers. Drillers are inherently drillers who tend to have large egos and can be narcissistic. Their unrelenting focus on self is so powerful that it is difficult for them to see the damage they cause to organizations, fellow team members, and others. They survive in organizations because they can be high-performing drillers, and managers erroneously think they can change them into high-performing sitters or rowers. But as we know, personalities are intrinsic and highly improbable to change. And while the skills of a particular driller may be very desirable, their unchangeable attitude and ongoing destructive nature will surely bring down an organization's productivity.

Rowers of Life

Of course, we can't escape the question: Do rowers row in all life experiences? As we view the concept of rowers, sitters, and drillers in the business world, we can't help but begin to see the parallel truth in all our other relationships.

Through this, we begin to see the rower as the individual who has an opportunity to attain self-actualization. The ability to leave the ego behind and focus on the common good for all humanity is an active awareness that can only be achieved through active participation in self-regulation and self-discovery.

Realizing our responsibility to be a rower of life is a human ambition, not just a business goal.

PART II

The Case for New Leadership in the Workplace

CHAPTER 3

Personalities and Behaviors

God grant me the serenity to accept the things
I cannot change, the courage to change the things I can,
and the wisdom to know the difference.
—Serenity Prayer

This chapter provides research and context pertaining to personalities and how these findings directly impact hiring and the ultimate success of any business. More to the point, the referred to body of research addresses the age-old debate of nature versus nurture. Are we the former, programmed from when we were a fetus to essentially be who we are today, with our personalities hardwired into our DNA? Or are we the result of the latter—born as blank slates molded by those who raise and surround us, influenced by the experiences from our formative years and what we consciously determine?

As touched on in the first chapter, the Positive Leader contention, supported by research, is that everyone's personality is formed by "nature" and continues to grow along that trajectory throughout that person's life. This is a vitally important consideration when embarking on a long-term relationship, which is what we hope for with any new hire.

Still, while reviewing work history, evaluating successes, and interviewing candidates, most organizations do not delve into their personalities beyond this initial observation. Some have even tried to add odd questions, such as asking the candidate to tell a funny story from their life or requesting more personal details. These are intended to glean insight into the candidate's personality but are ineffective and inappropriate. The typical interview process—sans the referred to odd questions meant to reveal more about the candidate—does not include any proven method(s) to reveal the ultimate success driver: personality traits that eventually contribute to a positive culture and organization. This is a grave miscalculation in the hiring process, as your employees' personalities will drive your business to success . . . or sink it.

How Organizational Behavior Impacts the Workforce

Organizational behavior studies the "why" and the "what" of a company's ability to be successful. The predominant focus is observing and instructing managers and leaders to motivate the staff to achieve its highest goals and increase production efficiencies.

Tied to this focus is the need to constantly elevate the quality of what is produced or provided as a service while also generating a lower employee turnover rate, especially among highly skilled team members. Most organizations refer to these accomplishments or experiences as their culture.

The overarching objective of any organization is to have a culture that attracts and retains happy, energetic, highly engaged team members who provide exceptional service and simultaneously eliminate disengaged individuals who destroy the positive culture and, ultimately, the organization's success. Yet according to Gallup's *State of the Global Workforce: 2022 Report*, an astounding 85 percent of the global workforce is disengaged. In the United States, the numbers fare slightly better, with 36 percent of the workforce reporting they are engaged in their work. These numbers are significant, as engagement is a leading indicator of productivity in any business, regardless of its location. In terms of financial outlook, a highly engaged workforce increases profitability by an astonishing 21 percent.

Although the numbers look grim, there is good news. Engagement is significantly impacted by employee recognition, with 37 percent of employees surveyed saying recognition was critical to their engagement on the job. While 37 percent may not appear significant, it points to the fact that this type of interaction is a tangible method employers can use to impact their bottom line—through engagement directly. Moreover, formally recognizing employees for good work takes a few moments but can yield instant and long-lasting positive results.

This ties in directly with the rower, sitter, and driller methodology developed by Positive Leader. Rowers thrive in work ecosystems where managers recognize their efforts in one-on-ones or provide praise in front of other team members. This recognition further motivates them to proceed happily down the path of productivity. When they perform admirably, sitters also benefit from positive praise, which gives them a sense of accomplishment and belonging. Recognition also serves a dual purpose with sitters, keeping them leaning toward the rower's work ethic. When a driller receives recognition for a job well done, it does not have the positive result it does with rowers and sitters. This is because no amount of praise is enough for a driller, as they lack respect for their manager's evaluation, believing they could manage the process better.

Some organizational leaders make the mistake of thinking they can wait until the organization begins to turn a profit or at least grows before they concern themselves with creating or maintaining an organizational culture. The reality is this wait-and-see approach is complicated for two reasons.

The first reason is drillers are hard to get rid of—not only because they will do anything to stay by blaming others but they usually have no other alternatives. This is because they don't possess a learning mindset and an empathetic personality. Because of these shortcomings, they are unlikely to be competitive in the market and thus will be unable to find a job. Ironically, it is your rowers who perform exceptionally well and can leave your organization quickly for a better work opportunity.

The second reason is that research suggests that building a positive culture early on is essential. Dr. Benjamin Schneider, a renowned educator and researcher of organizational behavior and organizational psychology, proposed the attraction-selection-attrition model. This model reflects that an organization tends to attract and select similarly minded individuals. This means a team or organization with a positive culture tends to attract and select similarly energetic, positive, and engaged candidates. Moreover, those who don't fit into this type of culture are more likely to quit. The opposite is also true. If an organization is unaware of the culture it has built or is building, it's highly likely that an average, or even a toxic, culture will result over time. According to Schneider's attraction-selection-attrition model, organizations will begin to attract and recruit uncompassionate, narcissistic, and selfish people. And sadly, those who are positive, engaged, and empathetic over time will likely leave the company. The result is an organization that is average at best and toxic at worst.

Starting a company—or even trying to reenergize a company—without first knowing what culture you want to foster is like building without a foundation. Building the culture you want with every hire is imperative from the start, and it is the only way to ensure forward momentum and avoid going back and starting over again.

The Link between Personalities, Behavior, and Results

Suppose we accept that personalities are generally hard to change, but behaviors can be taught and learned, as with a workplace skill set. In that case, this is where the most significant distinction lies in staffing evaluation processes and how the Positive

Leader methodology can have its most significant impact. Why? In a typical business environment, managers and leaders have minimal time to influence and motivate the staff. Most managers spend their days focusing on solving problems and fixing issues. They are error focused—what is wrong or not working, and how can the problem be fixed? It is the unfortunate truth about leadership, but spending the majority of time in crisis or "fixing" mode is a surefire way to create a disengaged workforce.

Remember: positive leadership focuses attention on what the staff is doing right, providing immediate feedback and praise, and determining what can be mirrored in areas where others may be struggling. The focus must be on the high-energy staff who excel in all their work areas. They not only produce quality products and services but they are also engaged, excited, and willing to share and learn.

The questions we should be asking are: Who are these people, and how can you get more of them?

The answers to those questions begin and end with how well you understand personalities and behaviors. Managers and leaders need to know and understand who to motivate, what behaviors can be modified, and the difference between the two.

Behavior versus Personality

Behavior is how an individual comes across to others in their actions. It can be modified, learned, and improved to meet the needs of specific tasks or responsibilities. The ability to perform skill sets is taught and therefore can be viewed as behaviors. Essentially, they are what we do.

By contrast, personality goes much deeper to the core of the individual; it is defined as the combination of the following attributes:

- values
- views
- set responses
- thought patterns

Collectively, personality is a relatively stable aspect of an individual. More importantly, personalities are inherent and take a long time to change, if at all. Simply put, they are extremely difficult, if not impossible, to change. There can be times of anomaly—when these characteristics stray from the norm. This is usually during times of intense stress or upheaval. After the stressor or event has passed, the personality generally returns to its previous state.

Personalities are who we are and why we act in a certain way while performing skills. Another way to look at personality is observing our attitude while performing tasks. This is seen day in and day out in all professions. In the medical field, for doctors, nurses, and other types of clinicians, it is referred to as "bedside manner." According to research studies, health-care professionals who show compassion and take the time to communicate with their patients produce more positive patient outcomes that affect patient satisfaction, compliance, and overall health status.

When you look back at working with others at jobsites, you

should be able to understand the role personalities play.

At one location, the housekeeping department decided that they would like to change their uniforms. This involved taking a survey of over three hundred team members. When we finally settled on the desired color and material, we ordered the uniforms, and the team began wearing their new uniforms. As with all decisions made, some of the team were not in agreement but acquiesced with the decision, and in the end, they were happy. Two team members, however, continued complaining and blaming others for making the wrong decision. They insisted management forced the decision and created a conspiracy theory around the decision. The same members complained about the new equipment, the new schedules, and the new sign-in process. Their complaint was focused on how it affected them, not how the team would benefit. They created an environment that kept the team from celebrating successes. Eventually, their negative focus led to their dismissal from the organization, but not without a tremendous amount of energy being used to maintain a positive culture. Once they were dismissed, the department flourished, and the team became stronger, producing higher quality, as witnessed through the third-party customer scores.

Where Does It All Begin?

As has already been alluded to, there have been numerous studies on how personalities are formed, with the debate of nature versus nurture being as old as ancient Greece.

The most famous of these studies, recorded and viewed as the definitive research of the "nature" aspect of personalities, are the twin studies conducted in the United States (in particular, in Minnesota), England, and Australia. In 1979 Thomas Bouchard, PhD, conducted a fascinating study of twins. Then director of the Minnesota Center for Twin and Family Research, Bouchard looked at identical and fraternal twins separated in infancy and reared apart. "The conclusion is that there is enough empirical evidence to convince anyone except the most extreme skeptic that virtually all human psychological traits are influenced by genetic factors to a significant degree."[1]

Personality scholars go on to identify the big-five personality traits as being:

- emotional stability
- agreeableness
- extraversion
- openness to experience
- conscientiousness

The twin studies reviewed the similarities and differences in personalities of identical twins who shared one fertilized egg, which split to form two babies sharing the same genetic soup, and fraternal twins, in which two eggs are fertilized with two sperm to produce two babies sharing only 50 percent of the genetic soup. This and subsequent studies have provided enough

---

1. Bouchard Jr., Thomas J., and Loehlin, John C., "Genes, Evolution, and Personality." *Behavior Genetics* 31, no. 3 (June 26, 2001): 243–73.

data and research to conclude that personalities are inherent, and the environment plays substantially little or no part in shaping them as the person ages. Some of these studies include Loehlin (1992), Jang et al. (1996a), Rieman et al. (1997), and Waller (1999). All provide research and data that indicate the heritability of self-report measurements of the big-five factors.

In the self-reporting by these fraternal twins who were separated at birth, the following reflects the inherited percentages of the big-five personality traits shared between the siblings:

- extraversion: 49–50 percent shared
- agreeableness: 35–51 percent shared
- conscientiousness: 38–53 percent shared
- neuroticism: 41–58 percent shared
- openness: 45–61 percent shared

The remaining percentages comprise a conglomerate of residual causes, such as nonshared environmental influences and chance factors in development, in addition to standard errors in measurement.

But why are these studies and their conclusions critical to workplace management and relationship development? The answer is relatively straightforward: The research strongly indicates that personalities are inherent and, it appears, less shaped by the environment, especially among adults. This means every time an individual is hired, they bring a set of personalities with a high improbability of being modified. Therefore, candidates, for all intents and purposes, are who they are.

To offer balance, this begs the question: Is there any hope

that personalities can be modified? Based on the following, the answer is minimal yet specific. "It has long been believed that people can't change their personalities, which are largely stable and inherited. But a review of recent research in personality science points to the possibility that personality traits can change through persistent intervention and major life events."[2]

A 2022 published meta-analysis by Bleidorn and colleagues shows that the potential for personality change occurs during childhood and adolescence. After about the age of twenty, the big-five personalities tend to change very slowly over a long period of time. In fact, traits necessary for positive leadership, such as openness to change, decrease over time. The bottom line: traits tend to change minimally over our lifetime (from twenty to eighty years old).

While consulting at a major health-care institution, I coached each manager and the front-line supervisors one-on-one.

We reviewed the training sessions for their staff's work responsibilities and discussed how to frame their recognition and how to introduce corrections on the job. One manager, who had thirty years of experience in a supervisory role, was quiet and disengaged during our session. She had completed a personality assessment, and I had reviewed the results before our meeting, and the results of that assessment were not aligned with her behavior.

I knew this supervisor had high levels of extraversion, compassion, and empathy. But the assessment showed she was

---

2. Nikos-Rose, Karen. "Scientists Say You Can Change Your Personality." ScienceDaily. (December 12, 2019). Retrieved January 23, 2024 from "http://www.sciencedaily.com/releases/2019/12/1912121659.htm" www.sciencedaily.com/releases/2019/12/1912121659.htm.

not a change agent and struggled with learning new ideas. So I waited for her to open up. Typically, people with high levels of extraversion cannot stop themselves from talking. In a matter of time, she began to express her feelings.

This supervisor was disillusioned with how she had performed her role in the past, leaving her silent. She felt she had wasted many years focusing on the "wrong" people—spending 80 percent of her time on drillers, hoping to change them. She also realized she had taken for granted the rowers—those individuals she knew she could count on.

I asked if her focus on the drillers changed them. She replied that it did not and that it took a significant amount of effort to move them out of the system. I then posed the question of why she would spend so much time on one or two people. Her answer reflected her high level of compassion. This supervisor explained that these specific employees were single moms who needed their jobs. She felt terrible that she would potentially have to fire them. Instead, she intended to get them to change. Unfortunately (but predictably), they did not, and she spent excessive time with human resources working through the process to terminate them. She explained that letting these employees go was extremely hard for her, and she felt guilty. But she went on to explain that now, knowing through the Positive Leader training, she had ignored her prized rowers and sitters in the process of trying to help those two drillers. This brought about more guilt for her.

This was a great example of how the best intentions can lead to the wrong business decisions. In focusing on the personal situations of a few employees, who were unmotivated to change, this manager had neglected her best employees, the rowers, and likely set back any positive momentum of the sitters. I explained that this was common and that her high levels of compassion kept her from seeing the bigger picture. The significant takeaway is that it is imperative to remember that, as Spock said in *Star Trek II*: "The needs of the many outweigh the needs of the few."

As a leader, your focus must be universal, not personal or individualistic. When the focus of attention is on one, especially on those who, due to their inherent personalities, are drillers, you inadvertently punish everyone. You focus on what is wrong by channeling your energy toward these drillers. Just as importantly, you do not show the power that comes from celebrating what others are doing right. This is the essence of positive leadership: recognizing what is right and sharing that with everyone. In response, your rowers and sitters will mirror that behavior and be inspired to produce the same results.

Behaviors and Skill Set

Behavior is a range of actions and mannerisms made by individuals, organisms, systems, or artificial entities within particular environments. It is how we act or conduct ourselves toward another or in response to a situation or a stimulus.

Behaviors can be encouraged through rewards and positive recognition or discouraged through punishment. It gets confusing when one tries to separate behaviors from personalities. A helpful example is when someone has a personality with a high degree of introversion and is asked to speak to a large crowd.

The "behavior" is the act of speaking to the crowd. Of course, they would experience a great deal of terror and anxiety in the process, but introverts can be successful as speakers. Most certainly, introverts will have to challenge themselves and prepare to produce the desired outcome for the speaking event, but in the end, they will remain introverts.

Skills such as correctly performing tasks can, over time, be modified and improved. We can see this in the medical field, where clinicians have learned to conduct exams or procedures with a high skill level yet still ignore the patient. This focus on knowledge while ignoring the human aspect of the job can be witnessed as being rude, unresponsive, and uncompassionate. In this example, the behavior of conducting a good exam or successful procedure is a skill; the lack of empathy is personality. Think of behavior as what needs to be accomplished and personality as how it is accomplished.

In his book *Outliers*, Malcolm Gladwell cites that people can achieve a high level of skill with ten thousand hours of practice. Gladwell's research for this contention was from K. Anders Ericsson's study of musicians who had all achieved high success. A common thread was that all had practiced for ten years, or approximately ten thousand hours. In his article "The Role of Deliberate Practice in the Acquisition of Expert Performance," published in 1993, Ericsson and his coauthor dove deep into what deliberate practice is. "Deliberate practice is a highly structured activity with the explicit goal of improving performance. It is practicing specific training activities, drills, and exercises designed to stretch the individual's skills and thereby provide growth."

In summary, training programs can be developed to modify

skills through practice and desired behaviors. Albeit, this change is complicated, as it involves the ability of a person to disrupt a current habit while simultaneously fostering a new set of actions. While we know we can successfully teach new skills and modify behaviors, we can see that much effort is required of the trainer and significant commitment from the student.

Personalities and Behaviors Influence Development

Let's begin with the research and information supporting the need for positive leadership and the concept of rowers, sitters, and drillers. First, it is evident through many studies conducted over the years that most, if not all, of our personality—the why of what we do—is inherent, and the environment has little to do with our ability to influence or modify our personality traits.

Next, we see those behaviors—what we do—can be modified, and an individual's skills can be improved with focus, dedication, and desire. Research also points to the influence of genetics on a person's ability to achieve high levels of performance with ten thousand hours of deliberate practice.

An excellent example of this involves any sport. To be able to perform at a high level in the world of athletics, it takes some inherited traits, to be sure. But it also involves practicing shots, throws, running patterns, and developing the proprioception that helps refine any good athlete. Even ice hockey star Wayne Gretzky—considered one of the best, if not the best, players in the history of the sport—would shoot tennis balls against the wall in his basement for hours on end when he was a child. Yes, he was born with an uncanny "ice sense" and a keen skill for the game, but he also put in tens of thousands of hours of training from when he was a little boy.

Behaviors also can be the result of inherent personality traits. One such trait, openness, is linked through research as a personality trait that offers a higher success rate in accepting change and bringing creativity to work. Individuals who possess openness prefer variety and diversity, and they seek new experiences and adventures, are curious about their environment, and have an interesting perspective on it. By contrast, less open people often avoid change and new events.

My experience as a hockey coach underscores these concepts and principles. For many years, I coached ice hockey at varying age levels. The skills involved in playing a complicated sport like ice hockey are numerous. The success of the players who go on to become professional hockey players is determined by their hard skills: stick handling, the ability to see the ice to make plays, the talent to shoot and pass the puck on target, and the pure athleticism needed to do all this while skating.

Studies estimate that one out of four thousand players make it to a professional ice hockey level. This can include playing in the NHL, one of its minor league affiliates, or other professional leagues worldwide. Typical factors of success seen in this group are

- they start young—usually by four years old;
- they have size—more prominent players are more likely to be selected in drafts and signed to contracts; and

- they capitalize on training opportunities to form good hockey habits.

In summary, good hockey skills equal good hockey behaviors on the ice, as evidenced by Wayne Gretzky's success.

In coaching hockey at a higher level, where the players were seventeen and eighteen, I began to see that certain players may have had excellent hockey skills, similar to managers who had gone through Q-School. Still, they lacked the relationship skills to participate in solid team performance. As mentioned in the previous chapter, it initially baffled the Positive Leader team when managers who were put through the same Q-School training exhibited different results. Ultimately, the personality component told the story of why two managers could go through the same education and yet show different levels of learning. This scenario also plays out in professional sports, where highly skilled and talented players can be cancerous in the locker room.

The following excerpt is from an article published in TheSportster.com on January 7, 2015, written by the TS staff, titled "Top 15 Worst Locker Room Cancers in NFL History": "The formula is downright simple: Bad teams with no locker room cancers are easier to build and root for than a talented team with one or two players who are so full of themselves, they divide team loyalty. We all know that if cancer is left unchecked, it can spread like wildfire. It is these headcases who make a name for themselves for all the wrong reasons."

The article goes on to explain that the only solution is to remove cancer: "I began to see that the only way the team would work as a team was to remove the players who exhibited high levels of egotism and would take credit for the team's success but would place blame on others for the team's poor performance." It matched up with my managers at the facilities they managed. When things went well, they took the credit, and when issues occurred, they would point fingers at others.

Turning these observations to the business world, I began to realize the inability of drillers to accept change. Why? Because they were so deeply rooted in their beliefs that learning was not an option.

The process began to determine which personality types were capable of having the desire to learn, change, and help others achieve higher levels of success by focusing on positive outcomes. As mentioned above, people with high levels of openness are capable of change and can be change agents who lead the desired change. Openness also indicates a desire to learn. These individuals tend to be people with an intrinsic desire to learn and a high learning mindset. An intrinsic desire to learn or a learning mindset refers to a passion driven by internal rewards that satisfy the learning individual. It is also vital to bring in individuals who are not egotistical or narcissistic—willing to share their success.

Another critical personality that has picked up steam in recent management scholarship is compassion, or the ability to care for another. This is usually seen as a personality trait reserved for those, for instance, in the health-care industry. True, while most employees in a typical business do not need to call on the type of hand-holding compassion that nurses, doctors, and other health-care providers use, it is still paramount in creating a positive work ecosystem, as compassion, including that conveyed to work colleagues, is vital in establishing trust in relationships.

At HHA, the above personality traits were present in the top-performing managers. And the third-party surveys provided evidence their staff and customers appreciated and respected them. Even more critical, they embraced the concept of a positive leader. They loved focusing on the strengths of the team and providing positive feedback. It was almost as if they were given permission to do what felt good, right, and natural to them!

Having learned through these experiences, the pathway forward for Positive Leader became clear. In order to change behaviors and improve skills, there needed to be solid programs, with attention focused on staff members who wanted to learn and accept change. It became apparent that focusing any attention on the drillers would produce failure in that their inherent personalities could not be modified, and this personality type created a natural barrier to their desire to learn or change.

Remember: even if a driller could be changed, it is not worth the time, work, and focus needed—and that's if the driller had an authentic desire to change. Again, it goes back to the eighty-twenty rule—spending 80 percent of the time with minimal, if any, results is not a productive use of anyone's time. And during the time of fruitless effort, the rowers would undoubtedly leave.

Based on all the data and practical experience, the Positive Leader team knew with unquestioned certainty that businesses needed science to help unlock the difficulties of the hiring process. And once applied, that process would point them to rowers, and they could then acknowledge the sitters and place red flags on drillers.

CHAPTER 4

The Power of Negativity

The ego creates the ripples of negativity.
—Osho

D
o you ever look at moments in your life and wonder where the time went, what you accomplished, and what you could have done differently? Do you see your mind concerned about what will happen, anxiety-ridden, fearful of future events, doubtful of what can be? When you plan an adventure or review an opportunity, do you become obsessed with what will go wrong and how you will fail?

Even in this age of significant technological advances, with opportunities all around us, people still feel drawn toward anticipating many possible obstacles or disasters that could befall them.

This focus on what could go wrong is a hardwired attraction to negativity. Focusing your attention on what is wrong and

65

what could go wrong is a natural habit and a biological trait from our prehistoric ancestors. The survival mechanism was inherited from the first humans who roamed the earth.

Every day our prehistoric ancestors woke up and spent the day trying to survive. Seeking happiness or reflecting on positive thoughts were not essential or even logical, as they could result in loss of life or limb. This truth has directed scientists to many explorations and discoveries, including American neuroscientist Paul MacLean, MD. In the 1960s, Dr. MacLean formulated what he called the triune brain model. He suggested that our lowest form of brain function, found in the basal ganglia, or brain stem, is all about pain avoidance as a means of survival. This can also be referred to as our primal instincts. Dr. MacLean called this part of our anatomy our reptilian brain, also known as the primal brain.

Likewise, Daniel Siegel, MD, has explored this line of research in depth, furthering the conversation of this primal brain form. In Dr. Siegel's book *Mindsight: The New Science of Personal Transformation*, he explains that the brain stem formed what some call the reptilian brain hundreds of millions of years ago. Here is how Dr. Siegel summarized the function of the reptilian brain and what it spawns.

The brain stem receives input from the body and sends information back down again to regulate basic processes such as the functioning of our heart and lungs. Beyond controlling the energy levels of the body through regulating heart rate and respiration, the brain stems also shapes the energy levels of the brain areas above it, the limbic and cortical regions.

The brain stem directly controls our states of arousal, determining, for example, if we are hungry or satiated, driven by sexual desire, or relaxed with sexual satisfaction, awake or asleep.

Clusters of neurons in the brain stem also come into play when certain conditions seem to require a rapid mobilization of energy distribution throughout the body and brain. This so-called fight-flight-freeze array of responses is responsible for our survival at times of danger. Working in concert with the evaluative processes of both the limbic and the higher cortical regions, the brain stem is the arbiter of whether we respond to threats either by mobilizing our energy for combat or for flight, or by freezing in helplessness, collapsing in the face of an overwhelming situation. But whichever of these responses is chosen, when we are in survival mode, our reactivity makes it quite challenging, if not outright impossible, to be open and receptive to others.[3]

Besides being a primer in neurology, the above passage from Dr. Siegel provides information on the hardwiring that contributes to each individual's response. Based on their personality, a person will respond with fight, flight, or freeze in addition to the situation. What is most significant is that when anyone is in survival mode, it is nearly impossible to hear or see what others might be proposing as alternatives. In the work environment, this is tantamount to a hard stop. Dr. Siegel goes on to explain

3. Siegel, Daniel J. *Mindsight: The New Science of Personal Transformation*. New York: Bantam, 2010.

that the brain stem, in conjunction with the limbic system, works to push individuals to act.

The next evolution occurred when small mammals first appeared around two hundred million years ago. Referred to as the "old mammalian brain," it worked closely with the brain stem and the body. This combination created not only our basic drives but our emotions as well. Dr. Siegel goes on to explain:

These feeling states are filled with a sense of meaning because the limbic regions evaluate our current situation. "Is this good or is this bad?" is the most basic question the limbic area addresses. We move toward the good and withdraw from the bad. In this way, the limbic regions help create the "e-motions" that "evoke motion," which, in turn, motivate us to act in response to the meaning we assign to whatever is happening to us in that moment.[4]

The limbic area also plays a crucial role in our relationships with others, allowing us to engage our emotions and attach them to another. This behavior is also seen in mammals other than *Homo sapiens*—think about dogs and cats and their connections with us. These furry friends have developed a mammalian limbic region, which allows them to connect emotionally with us and others of their kind. Not only does the limbic region make this connection possible but it encourages us to do so.

Dr. Siegel goes on to further explain the continual development of the brain—the cortex. The development of the cortex

---

4. Siegel, *Mindsight*.

marks the beginning of our increased awareness and the ability to think about thinking. The cortex gives us an even greater capacity to form and conceptualize ideas.

While all this is fascinating, it begs the question: Why is this important to relationship development and positive leadership?

First, it drives home the point that humans are built to react to fear, an automatic response that can take over during stress or panic. Understanding these basic neurological building blocks can go a long way in understanding how asking someone to react differently or telling them to stop acting in a certain way may be humanly impossible for them, based on their past or current experiences.

Second, the deep brain dive helps explain nearly every human being's focus on negative thoughts. The desire to seek out and linger in the areas of our life that can do damage or create errors is inherent. We seek the negative before we think of the positive because it is logical for survival, and this remains the most basic need we have as humans. As Roy Baumeister, PhD, an esteemed social psychologist, and his colleagues wrote:

> The greater power of bad events over good ones is found in everyday events, major life events (e.g., trauma), close relationship outcomes, social network patterns, interpersonal interactions, and learning processes. Bad emotions, bad parents, and bad feedback have more impact than good ones, and bad information is processed more thoroughly than good. The self is more motivated to avoid bad self-definitions than to pursue good ones. Bad impressions and bad

stereotypes are quicker to form and more resistant to dis-confirmation than good ones.[5]

Understanding all this better now, one can see how peo-ple naturally go to the negative first, as it is hardwired into our brains. Therefore, being an agent of change within the realm of developing a positive leadership mentality can be a challenge, to be sure. While many people have personalities that lean to-ward being positive first, the culture of most business environ-ments and our personal lives still centers on what is wrong or what could go wrong if things are left as they are. The ability for people to rewire this natural tendency in the workplace is challenging. But as the research supports, infusing positive en-ergy, rewarding successes, encouraging self-directed work, and practicing gratefulness all accelerate the overall achievements of a business and the individual.

Not only do we face these obstacles that challenge the hard-wiring of human beings but we also must confront the strong im-pact of negative bias because negative experiences, words, and outcomes stay with us longer than their positive counterparts. Again, for our ancient ancestors, there was no downside to for-getting a positive experience, but neglecting to pay attention to a negative one could result in dire consequences, even death.

The following quote provides excellent insight into negative bias and the unfortunate reality of its power:

---

5. Baumeister, R. F., Bratslavsky, E., Finkenauer, C., and Vohs, K. D. "Bad is Stronger than Good." *Review of General Psychology* 5, 4 (2001): 323–70. https://doi.org/10.1037/1089-2680.5.4.323.

Criticisms often have a greater impact than compliments. Bad news draws more attention than good news. Studies have shown that we remember bad experiences more than good, recall insults more than praises, react more strongly to negative stimuli, think and search out negative things more than good things. Sadly, we learn more from negative outcomes and experiences.[6]

Taking this concept a bit further and applying it to our work environment and other areas of our lives, it is apparent that negativity finds a comfortable home in pretty much any environment—in effect, breeding more negativity. The following provides an example of how negativity works like a virus if left unchecked: "People's moods are more affected by the coworker who gossips than by all the coworkers who are positive. Ultimately, this bias leads people to feel overwhelmed, resist change, and damage relationships."[7]

In the above-mentioned article, Drs. Mulqueen and Wolson discuss the two brain systems: One being emotional, unfocused, and automatic, also known as the lizard brain. The other is the rational, conscious, deliberate, and analytical neocortex. Their study explains that negativity bias inhibits people from positively changing their thinking and behavior, affecting their performance and dealing with stressors. Remember: drillers

---

6. Cherry, Kendra (2020). "What Is Negativity Bias?" Last modified November 13, 2023. Accessed January 24, 2024. https://www.verywellmind.com/negativebias-4589618.

7. Mulqueen, Casey and Wolson, Natalie. "Bias in the Workplace: Using Neuroscience to Improve Training." *Training Industry*. November 4, 2015.

are disruptive, creating an environment of self-attribution that focuses on what everyone else is doing wrong, effectively pointing the finger at others and, through intimidation, preventing others from pointing the finger at them.

While battling biology and hundreds of millions of years of genetic memory, how can a leader right the ship within their group of direct reports? How can an individual deal with drillers in their personal life? The only logical answer is to eliminate, or establish strong boundaries for, those individuals who drill into our businesses and lives.

In the workplace, implementing the Positive Leader philosophy and practice begins with and is anchored by insight into each individual's inherent personality via a personality assessment. Armed with this information, leaders know to whom they should direct their positive energy, knowing it will be well received. While negative bias is very real, it does not mean you have to live with it. Creating a positive work environment where you focus on what everyone is doing right allows these employees to tap into their very nature of positivity. You give them permission to explore their innate positive personality traits further.

When a positive leader can do all this, they foster an environment of creation and possibility. Positive leaders will guide employees to see their strengths by focusing on their successes. The outcome is precisely what any manager or leader wants: engaged employees, increased productivity, and lower turnover.

In our personal lives, drillers can be individuals who are a part of our families, friends, and others we encounter daily. The recognition that they are drillers may not become apparent because of our blindness to what we think our love should represent within these relationships. But remember: drillers are very good at convincing us they are correct and can be masters at manipulation. Just surviving in these types of relationships is not the answer. This may mean separating from drillers no matter what they represent in our relationships. This is a challenging, personal decision.

A Use for Negativity?

As you learn more about natural tendencies to lean toward the negative, you can understand that most management philosophies are issue-driven. Again, this goes back to human nature. Additionally, there appears to be a greater sense of accomplishment and a sense of "crossing things off the list" when errors are found, and the necessary corrections are made.

We can see the damage we cause in relationships by focusing on all the wrong things. Think about your most personal connection with your partner, spouse, child, or parent. If the main focus is on what the other person is doing wrong every day, how long would that relationship last?

John Gottman, PhD, determined through years of research that for every one negative comment made to a partner, it would take five positive comments to overcome the damage. This is known as the Gottman index of 5 to 1. On average, negative comments are five times more powerful than positive comments. Gottman studied relationships over the past thirty years, and through interviews of many couples, he determined their ability to have a successful relationship or if the relationship would end in separation. Gottman studied nonverbal cues and the framing of the comments about their partners during the interviews. Negative body motions, such as rolling eyes, crossing legs, folding arms, and other nonverbal negative cues, were studied and could predict failures in relationships long before they ended.

Although Gottman's focus was originally on the relationship analysis of married couples, it can also be applied to all relationships. The focus must be on understanding individuals' unconscious behaviors in day-to-day interactions.

Our greatest successes, highest productivity, and happiest teams focus on what they are doing right and mirror these efforts to strengthen positive outcomes.

Gain and Loss Framing

The concept of gain and loss framing ties in with that of negative bias and its power. Dr. Alison Ledgerwood and Dr. Amber E. Boydstun conduct one such body of research.

The research conducted by Drs. Ledgerwood and Boydstun found that the effects of loss framing linger longer than that of a gain frame. It also reflected that this asymmetry might arise because converting a loss-framed concept to a gain-framed concept is more effortless than vice versa. A gain frame is when you frame a message focused on a positive outcome; a loss frame is when you focus on the loss.

That said, gain framing is the opportunity to provide

feedback positively. Studies have shown that when gain framing is used in feedback situations, improvements are appreciated, and behavior is changed to meet the desired outcomes. In contrast, loss framing can trigger the individual to react angrily, and the correction is lost in an emotional response.

The key takeaways from the study were as follows:

- When behavior leads to a relatively certain outcome, then gain-framed messages work well.
- Gain-framed messages can be more persuasive than loss-framed messages when the outcome is clear and obvious.
- Human beings are more sensitive to minor losses than too little gains.

A practical example of gain framing in the business environment would be advising a staff member that improving their processes would lead to better outcomes, happier customers, and increased productivity. This would also lead to greater recognition for the staff member. An example of a loss-framing message to the employee would be that if you continue not improving your processes, you will be disciplined, which could lead to your termination. Gain framing emphasizes the positive results of adapting a recommended behavior. Loss framing stresses the negative consequences if they do not adopt a recommended behavior. Positive leadership focuses on positive outcomes as often as possible; however, even when a correction needs to occur, it is a strong preference to use gain framing to improve the skill level and behavior of the staff as opposed to loss framing.

In all our workplace relationships, gain framing is essential because it does not stimulate a counter negative response from the other. It can be framed as an inquiry, or it can be a reflection of self. Feedback and passing comments that are loss-framed can elicit a hostile reaction—natural protection to avoid pain, suffering, and embarrassment.

Again, it is a work in progress. This is not an easy shift, and we are working against millions of years of biological override.

CHAPTER 5

The Need for a Tool

If I had six hours to cut down a tree,
I would spend four hours sharpening the axe.
—Abraham Lincoln

Three individuals were hired simultaneously for different positions at a startup company in the business-to-consumer health-care industry. All three had entered a training program for a new management position. Each had the appropriate education but had different work experiences. The first candidate had minimal experience but was very energetic, and her former boss had said she was a fast learner. The CEO of the startup company was impressed with her enthusiasm and felt she would fit in due to her attitude. The second candidate had a lot of experience in managing but was outside the startup industry. He interviewed very well and received high praise from his former boss. The third candidate had the most expertise and interviewed very well. She appeared to be the best of the three.

Armed with this information, the CEO had to decide which candidate would be promoted to the new management position.

Deciding who to hire or promote based on interviews and past employers' recommendations is flawed. Many studies show that utilizing interviews alone in determining who will be hired or promoted can lead to costly results. And yet most organizations believe they can select the right candidate through interviews and checking past employers' recommendations. In most cases, the interviewers are unfamiliar with the job requirements and therefore ask the wrong questions. They tend to focus on negative information and make decisions within the first few minutes of the interview. Interviewer biases also play a role based on looks, manner of speech, ethnicity, and other traits. Back-to-back interviews create biases based on the interviewer's perception of each candidate at the moment of the interview. Finally, what is referred to as the "warm body syndrome," or the immediate need to fill a position, influences the interview process, tricking us into believing that we see something in a candidate that may not be accurate due to the self-imposed pressure to fill the position.

We also know that references from prior organizations and former bosses can be exaggerated or inaccurate. Most organizations will not provide accurate reviews of previous employees for fear of legal action or repercussions on social media.

Interviews can be effective in hiring or promoting if the questions are structured and consistent for each candidate when discussing skill levels. Identifying the soft skills and asking the appropriate questions without biases takes a lot of work to accomplish in the interview process. We also know from previous chapters that individuals with certain personality traits have more opportunities to succeed as leaders and managers.

The question became: How do we discover the personality traits in successful managers, and what traits were missing from the managers who could not produce the desired outcomes? The Positive Leader team leaned on several existing personality assessment tools to achieve the type of data they needed to proceed with a comfortable level of predictability. Working with a couple of universities and a company out of Canada, we began to identify specific traits of our successful managers and began formulating what an accurate assessment would possess to determine the necessary traits.

Personality assessments pose a series of questions to be answered. These are later aggregated using a finely tuned algorithm to provide an overview of the individual's authentic personality and resulting behaviors.

In this regard, we did not need the assessment to measure skill levels or business acumen; instead, they needed to focus, for example, on the individual's soft skills, such as compassion and empathy, and their ability to learn and adapt to change. These personality qualities and other traits are shown to predispose an individual's natural ability to form strong, healthy relationships and therefore become positive leaders.

The Positive Leader team was now getting a firm grasp on what would form the foundation of this hiring and employee engagement assessment. It would focus on the candidate's or current employee's core personality to gauge a future trajectory of success for that individual and, relatedly, for the organization's success. Without insight into this essential aspect of who the individual is, any efforts to engage them would be met with unpredictable results, which was unacceptable. The assessment is a valuable tool when utilized in the hiring or promotion process. Trained interviewers combined with a structured interview format increase the opportunity to select the correct candidate compared to just using an interview and recommendation.

Through years of testing different assessments, we realized we needed to create an assessment tool. The Positive Leader team wanted a tool to measure the various dimensions of an individual's personality that would lead to successful outcomes. We knew that certain personality traits were critical in this process. We began with what research has shown to be the essential traits of personality: empathy, compassion, and openness to change, to name a few. The research has shown that individuals with a high level of each trait excelled in establishing healthy relationships. In reviewing the successful managers within the company, we realized there were other traits they excelled in and aided in their success. These included their ability to accept and lead change. And the ability to communicate effectively, as Kim Scott refers to in her book *Radical Candor*, and the intrinsic desire to learn and continue learning. They must also possess a service attitude, be willing to serve humbly, and have high emotional intelligence. And finally, key behaviors that would come naturally, based on their personality, include gratitude, praise, and vision.

Let's go back to the three candidates in the above example. The decision of who would be hired would be left to the interviewing manager's hands. In most cases, no questions would be asked about the validity of the decision-making process. Now we know the flaws in this approach are very apparent, starting with

THE NEED FOR A TOOL

the manager interviewing. What do we know about the ability of this person to perform a structured interview? What is their current need situation? What types of biases does this person have that may be at play in the interview process? How has their success in their current position provided for them to accurately measure the success of the future candidate?

As we review the three candidates, which one has the skill to form strong relationships or the potential to develop a cohesive team? Which candidate can lead change or has the inherent desire to lead change in a caring and compassionate leadership style? Which candidate has the natural ability to communicate effectively to their team and their direct report?

How could these questions be answered in the interview process? How would the interviewer know the potential strengths and weaknesses of each candidate?

Assessments are tools that help organizations limit errors in the hiring and promotion process. The correct assessment executed properly and reviewed as part of the process eliminates biases, interview fatigue, and perceived intuition of the interviewer. Information gathered in the assessment can also help with future training and development.

CHAPTER 6

A Successful Leader's Traits

A genuine leader is not a searcher for
consensus but a molder of consensus.
—Martin Luther King Jr.

Often, as leaders, we become obsessed with leading. We see the future and create a vision and the associated goals that need to be reached to achieve that perfect vision. Then we fully expect everyone to follow us blindly.

It just doesn't work that way!

Managing and leading is a team sport. To achieve outcomes or goals, we must all have a shared vision. Optimally, it is a vision cocreated with our employees, providing them with ownership as well. At the very least, leadership's vision must be shared to enhance the sense of belonging for all involved. Even the most inspired and spot-on strategic plans will fall short if this is not handled appropriately. This is because mishandling the power of leadership leads to dissension, frustration, and an unwillingness to follow. In Simon Sinek's *Leaders Eat Last: Why Some Teams Pull Together and Others Don't*, he writes: "The true price of leadership is the willingness to place the needs of others above your own. Great leaders truly care about those they are privileged to lead and understand that the true cost of the leadership privilege comes at the expense of self-interest."

They must be able to provide positive energy every day, often putting their self-interest aside for the betterment of the company and the team. But not all team members are cooperative, and some may even be trying to sink the boat. Using effective communication every day can help overcome these potential obstacles.

The Role of Effective Communication in Success

If you ask any manager or supervisor what the most challenging part of their job is, they will unanimously agree that dealing with struggling employees through critical conversations ranks at or near the top of the list. Wouldn't it be great if your staff were perfect and all their work was accomplished without them raising any issues with the processes or with the behaviors of other team members? We can't expect that of ourselves, so it is fruitless to ask that of others. No one is perfect, and even the best employees sometimes make mistakes. So how do supervisors and managers create an environment more about learning and forward motion than criticism and "scolding"?

Our successful managers established a good working relationship with each associate; however, before getting there, consider the all-important question: What constitutes an excellent working relationship, and how can it be fostered?

Below are criteria that can help to establish a solid foundation in manager-associate relationships. These include

- getting to know your staff—their likes and dislikes; what motivates them;
- learning what their strengths are and then building on them;
- making sure each staff member understands how good outcomes are defined and measured;
- focusing on positive results every day and helping employees to build on them; and
- providing constant and constructive feedback.

As evidenced in the list above, the most critical criteria involve recognizing the positive. It is vitally important that your employees know what they are doing right. This begins and ends with the leader. You must initiate reflection, conversation, and interactions that focus more on what they are doing correctly than what they are doing wrong. Building this type of relationship establishes respect and trust between the manager and the associate. Looking forward, when the time comes to correct an undesirable behavior or outcome, it can be accomplished with minimal frustration. This is because the employee has repeatedly seen that you are more apt to recognize good work than work that falls short. This established trust is hugely impactful. After all, if the employee is to believe the positive recognition you have shared, they must also trust you when you offer constructive criticism.

Of course, the wrong way to go about helping your staff development is to do the opposite, which is only offering observations when something has gone awry or is being done wrong. Predictably, this approach results in the opposite effect—damaged relationships with employees, diminished trust, and no positive change.

When we focus daily on negative outcomes, we create an atmosphere of mistrust among staff members. If this is the majority of what they hear, they will feel that no matter what they do, it will not be good enough. We all have worked for bosses who believed it was their job to continuously find issues, running through them like a checklist and providing corrections interpreted as criticism. This leadership type knows that no one is perfect, but they still expect perfection. They honestly believe their role is to keep everyone "on their toes" to get the most out of them. In their book, to expect anything short of perfection is to concede to mediocrity. Obviously, this is far from the truth. People are not computer programs designed to spit out 100 percent accurate data all the time. Instead, any work ecosystem grows through empathy, coaching, and inspiration.

Equally troubling is the manager who ignores everything. These professionals provide neither positive nor negative feedback; they do not establish relationships and therefore do not understand their staff as human beings. In their book, everyone is equally to blame when issues occur, even though it was the manager's fault for not addressing them sooner. Instead of recognizing and shouldering this blame, these "leaders" will deflect by placing the responsibility on the group. This approach can come across as altruistic, as the finger isn't pointed at anyone. But the result is a lack of identification of the problem area; therefore there is no starting point to fix the issue.

Remember: every day is an opportunity to help your staff achieve *wow* service. This only occurs by being there *every day* to show gratitude and praise. Sometimes all it takes is a comment like, "Hey, good job on that project," or, "I was impressed by your work on that presentation." It does not take much energy to notice and say something. This sort of recognition, in turn, helps to establish continual positive outcomes.

Of course, we all know issues do occur, and as managers and supervisors, we need to conduct critical conversations for ongoing course corrections. These corrections should occur immediately when the issue is noticed or comes to light to achieve the most significant impact and the least amount of compounding problems. Some modifications are minor enough that a simple statement of what was wrong and what should have occurred can take place on location but in a private environment. Other corrections may require a more formal process. How these critical conversations are performed will determine whether you can maintain a healthy working and learning environment.

Communication Processes

Communicating isn't simply providing information and then listening to your staff. Correct communications involve critical aspects to ensure the message is understood and there is an opportunity for feedback.

First, some background. There are two basic types of communication: symmetrical, which aims to create a two-way, or bidirectional, dialogue, and asymmetrical, which is single-direction dialogue.

Symmetrical communication is a worldview and practice emphasizing "trust, credibility, openness, relationships, reciprocity, network symmetry, horizontal communication, feedback, adequacy of information, employee-centered style, tolerance for disagreement, and negotiation."[8]

By contrast, asymmetrical communication is a one-way, top-down approach designed to sway or control employee behavior according to management requirements.

Unsurprisingly, symmetrical communication leads to higher employee relational satisfaction. Leaders who practice symmetrical communication tend to be transformational leaders. This communication method simultaneously unites team members and dispatches the hierarchical model that has dominated the business world for decades.

---

8. Lee, Yeunjae. "Dynamics of Symmetrical Communication within Organizations: The Impacts of Channel Usage of CEO, Managers, and Peers." *International Journal of Business Communication* 59, no. 1 (2018): 3–21, https://doi.org/10.1177/2329488418803661.

Bernard M. Bass (1994), *The Future of Leadership in Learning Organizations,* confirmed the utility of transformational leadership for increasing organizational satisfaction, commitment, and effectiveness and the 6-factor model of the transformational-transactional factorial structure.[9] It has been defined by many as a leadership style that motivates followers by appealing to their higher-order needs and inducing them to transcend self-interest for the sake of the group or the organization. Transformational leaders tend to have high levels of compassion, empathy, relationship-building skills, and innovation. They are leaders who are rowers!

Studies have shown that transformational leaders take a genuine interest in the well-being of their employees. They foster a climate of trust and nurture confidence in their subordinates while at the same time encouraging individual development. Transformational leaders often interact closely with them to better understand and address their needs. In terms of decision-making, transformational leaders continually seek to empower followers. They are willing to share power and delegate significant authority to team members to make them less dependent on the leader. This type of leader inspires positive changes in those who follow, energizing the rest of the group.

These transformational leaders develop strong, independent-thinking, and empowered employees—people who trust their manager behind them and can then proceed with confidence. They become satisfied employees and loyal team members

---

9. Bass, B.M. "The Future of Leadership in Learning Organizations." *Journal of Leadership Studies* 7, no. 3 (2000): 18–40. https://doi .org/10.1177/107179190 000700302.

who contribute valuable contributions to the work.

In a transformational, symmetrical environment, information is consistently shared, transparent, and provided in team formats and one-on-one discussions. Leaders who practice these skills are willing to listen to their staff and receive feedback. At times, such feedback may reveal ways the leader can improve. Remember: relational satisfaction is a two-way street. Staff should feel comfortable providing feedback to leaders, and leaders should initiate open dialogue with employees for self-improvement. Some organizations use 360-degree evaluations to accomplish this through reviews from all three levels: their reports, coleaders, and bosses. Other organizations use one-on-one formats, providing monthly reviews between managers and direct reports.

In today's virtual workspaces and offices—and as increasing numbers of workers demand to work either 100 percent virtually or in a hybrid model—implementing tools to create team meetings and host one-on-one conversations through portals or web apps is perfectly acceptable. In 2020, when many industries and offices went virtual because of the COVID-19 pandemic, interactions via Zoom, Webex, or Microsoft Teams, for instance, were somewhat ineffective but necessary. But as leaders and workers grew into this virtual workspace, their skills at hosting meetings, participating in them, and remembering when to unmute or mute the microphone function began to improve. With that improvement and comfort level, the ability to share actionable feedback has also improved. While face-to-face meetings are still the most effective way to communicate, as they allow for more information to be disseminated through body language, eye contact, and tone, it is still better to host a virtual conversation than no conversation at all.

Emotional Intelligence in Leadership

Daniel Goleman, PhD, regarded as the father of the concept of emotional intelligence (EI), defines those with high EI as possessing "abilities such as being able to motivate oneself and persist in the face of frustrations; to control impulse and delay gratification; to regulate one's moods and keep distress from swamping the ability to think; to empathize and to hope."[10]

He divides EI into personal and social competencies. The personal competencies include

1. self-awareness—knowing one's internal states, preferences, resources, and intuitions;
2. self-management—managing one's internal states, impulses, and resources; and
3. motivation—emotional tendencies that guide or facilitate reaching goals.

The social competencies include

1. empathy—awareness of others' feelings, needs, and concerns; and

---

10. Goleman, Daniel. *Emotional Intelligence: Why It Can Matter More Than IQ.* New York: Random House, 2005.

2. social skills—adeptness at inducing desirable responses in others.

Reviewing each competency, we better understand the dimensions and how they help shape our leadership skills.

Personal Competencies

1. **Self-awareness:** Someone with self-awareness is considered to be introspective. They have the ability to notice and reflect on their internal state. If we are capable of looking in, we can clarify our core values, analyze our behaviors, work on our strengths, and initiate change to rectify our weaknesses. Research shows that people who practice self-awareness are happier and can form better relationships.

2. **Self-management:** Key components include the ability to self-regulate, adaptability, achievement, and positivity. Self-regulation is our ability to control our reactions, emotions, anger, and embarrassment. Years ago, when I was lecturing at a university, a discussion began on self-management, which can also be referred to as *self-regulation*. The question related to self-management centered on how good leaders can maintain a balance between their highs and lows. We address this by referring to the crests and troughs of a wave in a wave

tank. When the crests of the waves are incredibly high, and the troughs are shallow, it creates a roller-coaster effect. When succumbing to these crests and troughs as a manager, the result is that the staff rides along on that emotional roller coaster as well. Self-regulation is evident when the highs and the lows are not traumatic to the team. This is accomplished by recognizing the good times and correcting any issues with the slightest disturbance to the team. Leaders must be able to self-regulate. In doing so, they keep the waves' crests and troughs low and manageable—and away from their staff.

Another theory in management is the big wheel–little wheel analogy. Leaders are the big wheel, and attached to the cogs of the big wheel are the little wheels, represented by the employees. One turn of the big wheel spins the little wheel twenty times. Everyone's adaptability during these times is essential. From a leadership perspective, part of that adaptability is to remember the big wheel–little wheel cause and effect. At times like this, adaptability is critical in leadership to guide team members through those twenty spins or changes.

Great leaders or rowers are not only able to change course when necessary but they teach their teams to accept change as an opportunity. They practice organizational tacking, or the ability to successfully navigate change through all conditions, similar to sailing a boat. They know that all external forces must be considered before change can occur. They leave the door open at critical points to ensure the team and the organization can adapt. They are "change champions" for their team and the organization.

Leaders who are sitters struggle with adapting to change and therefore cannot lead their teams through change. Leaders *must* be change champions, striving to achieve and leading their teams to perform. Success leads to celebration, which leads to more success and greater creativity.

Finally, there are leaders and drillers who see achievement as a goal for their self-recognition. But the reality is, great leaders see personal achievement in the actions of others. Positivity or optimism is crucial in an effective manager, and each day is an opportunity to create. Teams need leaders who can and do provide positivity—that can-do attitude—so that creation can materialize.

3. **Motivation:** Everything starts and stops at the top, including motivation. Self-motivated leaders can provide an empowering and motivating environment by creating a safe space. Errors are learning opportunities, open and free communication, and trust is expected in both directions. It is critical to focus on what the team does well and not hunt for what it does wrong. Motivated teams are self-managed. They have what is referred to as positive regret. Positive regret helps us to self-correct. When we experience positive guilt for an action that is or is not taken, we learn from that mistake, and our chances of

creating the same error diminish. Leaders must learn to self-motivate. They must see the good—or positive regret—in what they do as a positive attribute, not a job that must be done. They must be able to rise above the discord and any negative views of others.

Social Competencies

1. **Empathy:** Empathic concern is the ability to sense what another person needs from you before they have to ask. There are three kinds of empathy we must consider if we want to develop into true universal leaders:

   » *Cognitive empathy* is when we recognize what someone is going through—what they may be feeling and what they may be thinking. Cognitive empathy helps us to understand what another is going through but keeps us at a distance from doing anything about the situation.

   » *Emotional empathy* is when someone else's feelings *become* yours, and you physically take on the emotions of the person experiencing their issue.

   » *Compassionate empathy* is when we *understand* a person's issue and choose to take some form of action to help that person.

   In health-care settings, studies have proven empathy shown by a care provider toward a patient can reduce the length of stay in the hospital, as the patient feels they have a partner in healing, someone who truly cares. This is the direct result of empathy. As we have learned, empathy is an inherent personality trait. The ability of a leader to practice empathy takes a minimal amount of time. And, unquestionably, leaders who can provide empathic concern for their employees form strong relationships. This can result in heading off issues through sense when situations are stressful.

Research presented by neurosurgeon Dr. James R. Doty, MD, at the inaugural Compassion and Healthcare Conference shows that health care delivered with kindness not only reduces the duration and severity of the common cold but can also lead to improved patient outcomes, including faster-healing wounds and a reduction in pain and anxiety. In some instances, the statistical significance of kindness-oriented care on improved outcomes was "larger than the effect of aspirin on reducing [a heart attack] or smoking on male mortality."[11]

2. **Social skills:** These are reflected as an adeptness at inducing desirable responses in others or relationship management. Working as a coach and mentor, inspiring, influencing, and conflict management are all part of leadership skills in managing relationships. Leaders are

11. Doty, James R. "Scientific Literature Review Shows Health Care Delivered with Kindness and Compassion Leads to Faster Healing, Reduced Pain." Presentation at the Inaugural Compassion and Healthcare Conference, Stanford University School of Medicine. November 12, 2014. Accessed January 24, 2024. https://www.dignityhealth.org/about-us/press-center/press -releases/scientific-literature-review-with-stanford.

called upon to manage as well as lead. A good leader and manager will provide inspiration through their actions and through their integrity. They coach when necessary, providing ideas, clarity, and focus. They mentor employees to become future leaders or to move on to other dreams. They see their team as individuals who are part of a collective. By meeting the needs of each, the effective leader allows the team to become stronger, showing how it can work harmoniously for the greater good.

In summary, a number of different studies argue that EI is a critical component of effective leadership. Some suggest that leaders high in EI are able to recognize, appraise, predict, and manage emotions in a way that enables them to work with and motivate team members.

Others propose that EI is "essential to effective team interaction and productivity and that the team leader's emotional intelligence is important to the effective functioning of the team. The leader serves as a motivator toward collective action and facilitates supportive relationships among team members. The emotionally intelligent team leader also provides a transformational influence over the team."[12]

The key is in the awareness of others. When we can place ourselves in another's position, we practice cognitive empathy. Leaders who can connect with their staff

---

12. Melita Prati, L., Douglas, C., Ferris, G. R., Ammeter, A. P., Buckley, M. R. "Emotional Intelligence, Leadership Effectiveness, and Team Outcomes." The International Journal of Organizational Analysis 11, no. 1 (2003): 21–40. Accessed January 24, 2024. https://doi.org/10.1108/eb028961.

at a higher emotional level create a relationship based on achieving the organization's overall success and less on individual goals. Leaders who score high in EI provide clear messages to their teams. They allow interaction and are not intimidated by challenges to their goals or their leadership. They want to develop future leaders more than just getting the job done.

The greatest lesson I learned as a new supervisor was taught to me by my employees. They were self-motivated when provided with respect and an opportunity to understand the overall mission and the goals established to achieve that mission. It is human nature to feel better when we are given the opportunity to think independently or "consult" on a strategy or change under consideration or in process.

In the end, the role of the leader should not be taken lightly. There are many stories of leaders promoted because they were the best at a particular skill needed to accomplish a role. Focusing on skill sets and behaviors to determine who will be a good leader can be disastrous. Leaders, it can be argued, are born, not created. Their positive traits are inherent and predetermined at birth. Under the right circumstances, they can hone these attributes to become better leaders, but they were born to lead. Highly skilled people are sometimes necessary to lead certain teams, to be sure. But in the long run, teams need leaders who are energizers, who have compassion, empathy, and love emanating from their hearts, and who channel all this into what they believe.

While watching the 2022 Stanley Cup playoffs, my wife, Debra, posed an interesting question. She asked if it were possible for an NHL coach to be successful if they never played the game at a high level. The perfect example is Jon Cooper, head coach of the Tampa Bay Lighting. Coach Cooper never played college or semipro hockey, let alone in the NHL. Despite this lack of professional on-ice experience or skill as a player, he is one of the most successful modern-day coaches, leading his team to consecutive Stanley Cup victories in 2020 and 2021—then back to the finals in 2022.

Ryan McDonagh, a defenseman with the Lightning—considered one of the top players at his position—had this observation about Coach Cooper's success, despite never having played the game at a high level: "He's not blustery. He's not going to pretend to be something he is not. What Cooper does well is articulate and motivate. He's just got a great way of communicating things in layman's terms, not trying to get too caught up in analyzing things."[13]

Coach Cooper brings honesty and integrity to the table and also excels at communicating with his audience—the twenty-plus players in the locker room who take what he says onto the ice. Now that is an effective leader!

The goal of the Positive Leader was beginning to unfold: help

---

13. Romano, John. "Jon Cooper teaches. He motivates. He delegates. Mostly, he just wins." *Tampa Bay Times*, July 4, 2021.

organizations find candidates, evaluate with the PAT[sm], and hire the individuals who, through inherent personality traits, would have the best chance at successfully developing healthy relationships.

We have discussed leadership development and the desire to create a strong organizational culture. But leaders and those who work in organizations are humans, individuals working together to create great products or services for others. They are all equally responsible to each other and to those they serve. There are rowers, sitters, and drillers in all areas and levels of our organizations. As members of our organizations, communities, and families, we should always be working to develop better skills.

When I think of relationships, I like to think of a series of rings that revolve around everyone. The innermost ring is composed of those who are the closest to us. They may include family members, relatives, and close personal friends. Most relationship studies describe them as intimate relationships. The next circle out from us could be identified as friends who we may see regularly but we may not view as part of our intimate inner circle. The third ring out is identified as people we participate with semiregularly. This may include friends we see intermittently and we know them through association. The outer ring is identified as individuals we interact with in our daily, weekly, and even monthly lives. Think of the mailperson, your mechanic, the people at the stores you frequent, or the staff who serve you at the restaurants you visit.

Each one of these relationships involves a connection to us on different levels. We tend to open our lives and share differently with each ring of our relationship. But through a higher awareness of self and others, we can begin to understand that all connections are an essential part of our lives at all levels. How we treat people across the spectrum of our rings influences our joy, success, and to a large degree, our ability to love.

Research has confirmed that who we are is determined by our ancestors' inherited physical and personality traits. It is obvious that physical characteristics are visible and cannot be manipulated by others; however, the personality traits that are a part of our inheritance can be manipulated through our environment. That is not to say personality traits can be changed, but we can be influenced and even manipulated to produce behaviors we are not comfortable with. Relationship development focuses on uncovering our true personalities and understanding why we may be uncomfortable in certain circumstances that may even cause anxiety.

Many of us have witnessed in our lifetime the alcoholic family member who became sober through treatment. My first experience was with an uncle. We would spend a lot of time together when I was young, helping him with gardening and listening to his stories about his job or what was happening in the world. He was kind when he was sober. His drinking would ultimately kill him, but during his life, he would fade in and out of his addiction. In the 1960s and 1970s, we didn't know that alcoholism would later be identified as a personality disorder and hence a disease. What would have happened to my uncle and many others if we could have communicated with them the cause of their disease?

That is the focus of Positive Leader—identifying the inherent personalities of individuals and providing them with the opportunity to understand why they are uncomfortable exhibiting certain behaviors, which will create stronger personal relationships and enable them to become the rower they can be. Through the review of our personalities, with the use of tools such as assessments, we have this opportunity. Then the definition of *rowers*, *sitters*, and *drillers* becomes clearer. It will help us recognize the drillers at our work or in other areas of our lives and understand and be able to change them. It will also allow us to see and appreciate the rowers, not take them for granted and provide them with endorsement. And in the endorsement of the rowers, the siters will become positively active.

PART III

Applying Rowers, Sitters, and Drillers in the Workplace

CHAPTER 7

The ABC of Relationships

There can only be a relationship between human beings
when we accept what is, not what should be.
—Jiddu Krishnamurti

The importance of establishing productive relationships in the workplace cannot be minimized. As a leader, a strong connection with your staff is vital to creating a positive culture and team committed to the high-quality services or products you're responsible for developing. Establishing healthy relationships is just as important when building trust and finding the ability to work through issues that may arise while doing business with your organization's customers. Importantly, this must be an active process in which you constantly review and adjust throughout your business and personal lives.

Many tools are available in the business world to establish

healthy relationships, and we will explore a few that we find work well in subsequent chapters. But first let's spend time breaking down the different parts of the relationship model.

In relationship development, the first step should be understanding ourselves. According to Socrates, "To know thyself is the beginning of wisdom." But the effort involves keen self-awareness. Plato also alluded that understanding "thyself" would help us understand human nature. He goes on to offer that the result of knowing ourselves would enable us to understand each other. From the moment we are born to the moment we die, we are inundated with others' perceptions of who we are, who we should be, or what we think we need to be based on the reflection of others. Our image of who we are is an external creation produced by misdirected love or by the manipulative actions of another.

As we have learned through research, our personalities are inherent and mostly set for life. Then we are heavily influenced by the external world to be what we should be, creating a trapped image. And to make matters worse, some are admired and praised, endorsing the idea and creating an ego that may influence how we form our relationships.

The *Suda*, a tenth-century encyclopedia of Greek knowledge, states: "The proverb is applied to those whose boasts exceed what they are, and that 'know thyself' is a warning to pay no attention to the opinion of the multitude."[14] We must recognize the self as an evolving concept free from external impressions.

In my studies and work with the Dhyan Vimal Institute for

---

14. The *Suda*, tenth-century Byzantine encyclopedia dictionary, circa 950 CE.

Higher Learning, I was introduced to what I will call the relationship formula. Dhyan Vimal, who is a scholar and author of many books on higher learning, created the formula. The intent is to express an understanding of what takes place in the development of relationships.

As we know, our ability to see ourselves is difficult due to environmental influences. Therefore, the opportunity to see ourselves is through a relationship with another; however, this is not easy. Vimal explains, "There is no way to know oneself just by oneself. It can only happen through all kinds of relationships through which you are revealed. In the revelation of you, you are not limited just to be this, just to be this you, for the first-time transcending becomes possible. Without the mirror, the sight of how one is never happening, and by this, most live out an assumption and mind-state of the self, and this misleads oneself and one's life. The ego becomes the only reality."[15]

Vimal's relationship model I am presenting will outline what should occur in the meeting of two individuals or in the review of an issue.

The formula, or model, is as follows:

$$\begin{bmatrix} a \overset{c}{\text{------}} b \end{bmatrix}$$

A (I)

---

15. Dhyan Vimal, series of lectures, DV Institute for Higher Learning, 2023.

The formula begins in the brackets, with *A* representing who we believe we are. Who we are is set at that moment, influenced by internal factors, such as our genetics, and external factors, including but not limited to those who have influenced us. Who we are is not necessarily correct, leading us to the *B* within the formula. The *B* represents the other person—a customer, an employee, and sometimes even an issue. The formula has an arrow between the *A* and the *B*. The formula represents the action and the communication that takes place between *A* and *B*. What occurs within this interaction is essential in the establishment of the *A*.

As Vimal explains, if the *A* has no self-identity, they allow themselves to be overtaken by the *B* or the issue. This occurs with individuals who have uncontrolled emotional empathy, compassion, and emotional intelligence. They will allow themselves to be controlled, or even manipulated, by others. This can occur intentionally or unintentionally. Suppose the *ego influences the A*, with high levels of intimidation and low levels of empathy, compassion, and emotional intelligence. In that case, the *A* can overtake or even ignore the other individual (*B*), misjudging the issue altogether. Why is this important in our workplace? We must be aware of the following as we establish our day-to-day relationships: Awareness of the other (*B*) in relation to our self (*A*) can determine the outcome's success. If we enter into a negotiation, for example, with the attitude that we know more than the other or are a more skilled negotiator, we might miss an opportunity to create a better outcome. This attitude could also lead to a prolonged negotiation or even a disastrous result that could influence future negotiations and the trust between the organizations.

Over thirty years with our health-care company, we had acquired businesses throughout the United States. As a service provider, when we acquired the business at each facility, we also took on existing staff and the existing union, which meant we would be responsible for future negotiations at each location. This required a keen negotiating ability since we needed to arrive at a fair negotiation with the union representing the staff and the facility we contracted the service with. Therefore, the union negotiation could determine whether we would continue our future agreement with the facility. One particular negotiation was with a union representing several of our sites throughout the United States. The talks were not only crucial for the current agreements at each of the six locations; we needed to establish a healthy relationship with the union management that would aid in future negotiations. Everyone at the negotiating table needed to understand the relationship formula. When negotiations began, it became evident that a senior member of our team may have had preconceived negative ideas toward the union. In the first few days of the talks, this individual created an atmosphere of tension and misdirection. When confronted in private, they explained that this was their strategy. They felt that through intimidation and chaos they would control the union negotiators.

Whether or not they would be considered a driller based on the assessment results, in this situation, they were definitely drilling. Their ego was destroying the opportunity to establish a cooperative negotiation. Information was also getting back to the facility administration, jeopardizing our agreement. Since I was the lead negotiator for our management side, I set up a one-on-one meeting with the union lead negotiator. I informed them that we had removed the person from the negotiating team. This action alone created the beginning of a fast and equally fair negotiation. Trust was established, and we could resolve the difficult issues with respect.

Let me clarify: not all negotiations had a similar outcome based on removing an intimidating negotiator. Some negotiations were extremely difficult, no matter what course of action we took. But through hundreds of negotiations with six different unions, creating an atmosphere of respect, and keeping an open mind to understand the intent of the other (B), we succeeded in all our negotiations. And in some cases, as with the Laborers International Union, I became the cochairperson representing management for the union management health and welfare fund and the service contract training and trust fund for twenty-three years.

Our roles as individuals, both A and B, are influenced by our environment. We are caught in a world of comparison. Labels that are religiously, politically, and socially, to name a few, applied to us in the course of our life make it easier for people not to have to work so hard in developing a relationship with one another. We don't have to accept each other if our labels are different; therefore we do not establish relationships that could have value, that provides us with reflection, that can help us grow into better leaders, workers, and humans. Vimal offers this insight: "We begin by being aware of another. Do you know the moment we are aware of another, we can never wrong another? You know, you can only be wrong when you're unaware."[16]

---

16. Dhyan Vimal, series of lectures, DV Institute for Higher Learning, 2023.

The opportunities that can be created between *A* and *B* are endless. When we represent *A*, we must set aside our ego and have an actual meeting, unrestricted by who we think we are, what others have placed on us, or what we believe the outcome should be. This allows *A* to truly see *B*, whether it is a person or an issue. Vimal explains, I am, you are, we are, I look at you and realize we are here, there is a space in between (*C*), only then the real [I] happens and the *A* becomes. The ability of *A* to witness themself is through the reaction of the other (*B*). But this can only occur when we can provide space to witness our response, calm our minds, and accept what is real. He refers to this space as *C*, identified as the formula's denominator. It can also be the pause before anger, before the argument, before we react, which are within our control, and yet we allow these failed emotions to consume us. In our pause, we can settle the mind, providing space to see what is the true intent of the situation that lies before us. Then the action is pure, and in the true sense of the meeting, *A* can become one with *B*, and *B* becomes *A*. In other words, there should be no separation so we can see what the true relationship is or the true situation.

The space, *C*, represents the opportunity cost of all relationships. If we choose to be absorbed by *B* or ignore *B*, the opportunity cost is losing what can grow from the relationship and our self-development. Developing the patience to create the space is a form of behavior modification. Counting to ten, asking for time to think through a situation, and providing positive feedback through repeating the conversation in an inquiry—also known as active listening—all create a new habit, leading to modified behaviors. Patience allows us to discover.

Over the course of my work experience, I have experienced frontline supervision, management of departments, divisions, companies, and countless consulting of other organizations in almost every industry. The value I have witnessed in the utilization of creating a space (C) within the different relationships and the issues that arise has been tremendous.

A great example occurred in southern Texas. Through a very rigorous proposal process, we were awarded a contract with a hospital system. The contract involved the management of over two hundred service department workers, operating over three shifts. We introduced new management into the department and promoted supervisors from within the existing staff. Extensive management training took place, and our goal was to increase the quality of service while maintaining current staffing levels. During the review of the work assignments and scheduled service times, we noticed that the first-shift workers, who were scheduled to begin work at 7:00 a.m. each morning, arrived at their scheduled areas fifteen minutes late each day. To our management team, this seemed like an easy fix and an opportunity to increase production. The immediate response was to inform the group that it is mandatory for them to be at their assigned locations at 7:00 a.m. After two weeks of arriving to their assignments on time, they began to show up late. The immediate response from the management team was to punish the members who were late through a written discipline. The problem, however, was compounded; there were over thirty people who worked this shift, and every one of them was late. The discipline process would take long, involved human resource review and could lead to us having to terminate the entire staff. Our reaction was without thought of what the intent was of the group for having a reason to be late to their workstations. In the relationship model, our A was more important than their B, and we were using power to produce an outcome. Although at first glance we would all agree that if you sign up to work the first shift, which starts at 7:00 a.m., you should be at your location at 7:00 a.m. But when an entire team doesn't show up at 7:00 a.m., you have to pause (C) to find what is the reason. We gave this opportunity to resolve this situation to a supervisor who was promoted from that very team. It was through her understanding of the team that she was able to provide a solution that would work for everyone. The team was comprised of all Hispanic workers who knew each other through relations and or lifelong friendships. Each morning, when they gathered to pick up their equipment, they would enter long conversations about their families and events. It was their opportunity to catch up and, in some cases, the only opportunity. The solution was simple. The supervisor suggested they take their first fifteen-minute break at the start of the shift instead of at the normal scheduled break time of 9:00 a.m. By acknowledging this important social occasion to the staff, they responded with arriving to their locations on time at 7:15 a.m., and their production and quality went up as a result.

By creating space (C) to determine the reason way others act the way they do, or why issues occur, we can reach an understanding that may not only resolve conflicts but indicate a respect for what others believe to be their truth. This respect not only produces a stronger relationship; it tightens a bond of trust between leadership and their staff.

What happens when the A becomes the true form of me, without comparison to others and the influence of the external world? I witness myself and become conscious of who I am consistently. This is represented in the formula by the A (I) to the left of the brackets. It is what is called the state of I am. I witness B, and through this witnessing of B, I become conscious of myself. Vimal explains, "So, in a deeper sense, in all relationships, the reality of the A, B, and C is more about oneself than the other. Only when one happens to be aware of oneself can the real meeting of the other or one's life happen actually."[17]

Many scholars have written about the conscious awareness of ourselves. Gurdjieff, in his book *In Search of Being*, refers to the seven levels of development. He identified that we cannot become self-aware until we reach the fourth level. The first three levels involve the physical body, emotional functions, and logical and intellectual correctness in that order. If we can get beyond these levels, we can begin to know ourselves and where we are going. Awareness of self begins.

The development of the self is critical in all relationships. Our focus needs to be directed inward, accepting our strengths as an opportunity to build solid relationships and to help others, as well as accepting our weaknesses as an opportunity to discover what we need to do to improve the outcomes in our lives.

The struggle against negativity will always be present, and we will have to battle the default mechanisms within our DNA that focus on what can go wrong, how we will fail, and the comparisons of ourselves to others. We must always be aware that

---

17. Dhyan Vimal, series of lectures, DV Institute for Higher Learning, 2023.

this can fall apart when we make our personal issues the universal truth or someone else's truth.

Let's review how the relationship model works within the concept of our rowers, sitters, and drillers model. Rowers bring an openness to all relationships. They respect the other (B) naturally due to very specific personality traits, such as empathy, emotional intelligence, perspective-taking, and compassion mixed with humility and the ability to communicate effectively. Take for example the supervisor at our facility in southern Texas. She was promoted not only due to her high skill set but because she possessed the positive attitude of a rower. Her ability to be able to understand the needs of both the organization and the staff solved the issue. And in the process of solving the issue, it improved the quality and increased production because the team felt respected and became more engaged. Rowers row organizations forward through positive relations, which include the ability to respect the other (B) and create the space (C) to arrive at a mutual resolution.

On the other hand, drillers enter the relationship or view the issue with a preconceived notion that they know better, that their perception is always correct, and that the other is to be a part of their goals and desires. Their position is one of self-gratification in all relationships and all situations. They can be dynamic and convincing. In the case of the above issue at the Texas location, a driller's approach would be to continue insisting the workers showed up at the location at 7:00 a.m. They would be willing to create an us-against-them environment, convinced they are right and everyone else is wrong. Due to their egotistical personality, they would not be able to see the issue from another perspective.

And lacking in empathy and compassion, they would be willing to terminate the staff who didn't follow their rules, unconcerned about the overall negative effect it would have on the department.

Sitters represent the majority of the workforce. They may not take a position in negotiations or relationships, and they can be swayed to agree or may completely avoid arriving at a conclusion in decisions. In the case of the Texas facility, prior management did not address the issue. Their inaction may be their view of acting, hoping the issue will resolve itself.

The work of a leader is to engage sitters and provide them with a healthy, safe space. Sitters who are properly managed can sometimes become rowers, and if not properly managed, they can be swayed by drillers and, at times, drill.

So how do we help individuals understand how their personalities and subsequent behaviors will influence their ability to form healthy relationships? The ability to see oneself (A) and to understand others (B) is accomplished through assessments, as we have mentioned in early chapters. Science and practical application has shown that through assessments we can determine communication styles, personality and behavioral strengths and weaknesses, and inherent personalities that lead to subsequent behaviors. When properly reviewed, these assessments can give us an insight into why we struggle and/or excel in some areas of our behaviors toward others. They also provide us a glimpse as to why rowers row, sitters willingly sit, and drillers choose to drill—tools that are vital in our workplace to help determine potential positive leaders. The next seven chapters give us a closer look at those behavioral areas in the workplace so you can leverage that knowledge.

CHAPTER 8

Creating the Path of Organizational Change

Change is hard because people overestimate the value of what they have—and underestimate the value of what they may gain by giving that up.

—James Belasco and Ralph Stayer

Having been involved with many organizational transformations throughout the past thirty years, I have developed a process that has yielded positive results. And as you will see, organizational change is directly connected to our concept of rowers, sitters, and drillers. How can we create the most efficient organization without the positive influence of rowers at all levels of the organization? Rowers, as individuals, are change champions, always seeking a better output in all they do at work and in their lives. Since organizations are comprised of individuals, let's begin by understanding the ability to modify behaviors in us as individuals. Through this understanding, we can apply the same principles to organizational change. When new positive behaviors are practiced, new habits are formed. Over constant repetition, we can create new neural pathways that become a part of our brain. This is also known as neuroplasticity:

> Neuroplasticity also called brain plasticity or neural plasticity. Neuroplasticity is the ability of neural networks in changes in the brain growth and reorganization. This change in brain ranges from the individual neuron pathways and makes new connections to systematic adjustments like cortical remapping. Examples of the neuroplasticity include circuit changes and network changes which result from learning a new ability, practice, psychological stress, and environmental influences.[18]

This is one of many studies that provide scientific proof that through learning and practice, we can create new neural pathways in our brains. But behavior modification is not as easy as flipping a light switch; it takes effort over a very long time. Think of practicing to become a better artist or athlete. Developing perfection in painting or performing a perfect ice-hockey slap shot involves many hours of painting or shooting a puck. In his book

---

18. Atkinson, Charlie. "Neuroplasticity: Neural Networks in the Brain." *Short Communications* 8, no. 3 (March 25, 2021).

Outliers, Malcolm Gladwell suggests at least ten thousand hours of practice to reach perfection. And even that is not a guarantee we will overcome prior behaviors and habits formed over a lifetime. It is the individuals within the organization who can either create or hinder its growth and success. As we have reviewed in previous chapters, we need to focus on the individuals who will design and advance the organization to its full potential.

Within dynamic organizations where improvements are championed, it is an organization that celebrates the rowers. The rowers set the energy, and the rest of the team follows. Sitters become rowers excited to be a part of a successful organization. On the other end of the spectrum, drillers will avoid change because it will take the focus away from them. They slow potential improvements by analyzing the change to its detriment, holding onto the current state if it has provided personal satisfaction. In most cases, they will not support change that will affect them in any way.

Moving beyond the current state of an organization is a living process. The detail of each timeline step will be outlined in the subsequent chapters, and I have provided a summary below to introduce the steps necessary to navigate the path. Let's begin our journey.

The first step involves a review of our existing state and the effects of the past.

Creating the Path of Organizational Change Timeline

Our Existing
State/The Effects of
the Past

The timeline illustrates the start of organizational change. The first step involves a review of past processes in all areas of the operation. This allows us to question all the decisions that have taken place over the years to determine how we arrived at our current state. To move forward, we must address the past, which involves reviewing programs, services, schedules, production capabilities, staffing, budgets, and other operational systems. Soft skills should also be examined, such as hiring practices, employee engagement processes, benefits, training and development, and other processes that help drive culture.

An organization's current state can be successful and provide satisfactory customer and company outcomes; however, other companies will ultimately produce better products or services as technology changes, leaving the organization in a state of reaction and potential failure. We also have to consider that operational systems are constantly evolving. International partners create time zone issues, remote work, and flex schedules challenge traditional management structures and corporate culture. Businesses need to be dynamic now more than ever.

The second step involves the evaluation of the current reality of the organization as it relates to both the internal and external environment.

Once we have successfully reviewed the past processes, we must evaluate the organization's current reality in relation to all areas that influence the company's internal and external success.

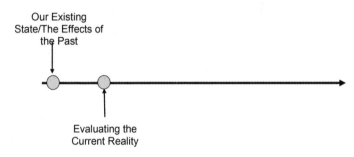

Creating the Path of Organizational Change Timeline

Our Existing State/The Effects of the Past

Evaluating the Current Reality

A SWOT analysis (strengths, weaknesses, opportunities, and threats) can accurately assess an organization's current state. This is a difficult stage of our path. To accept what is truly happening within the organization, we must be willing to acknowledge that up until this point, we may have been operating in a bubble, not recognizing what is really occurring in the organization's life cycle.

The third step involves implementing change.

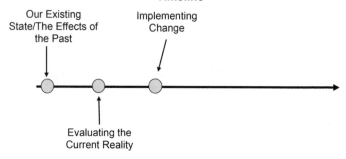

As we continue through the timeline, our following process involves implementing change. Including establishing a decision-making process that will aid in consensus going forward. What we say yes to and no as a group creates accountability at all levels. This step includes removing choices that affected us from our past experiences. It also consists in establishing new processes with each decision. The de-hassle format is a recommended process for establishing decision-making.

The fourth step involves developing consistent performance.

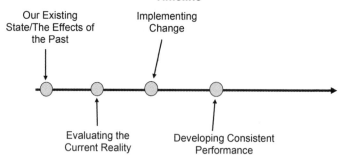

As we continue on the path of change, we must be aware that we can never be satisfied with what we have accomplished. This can occur at any moment within the process. In sports, it is called taking our eyes off the ball or fumbling. First, understanding the knowing-doing gap is essential in creating consistent performance. Then utilizing tools like one-on-ones to provide ongoing performance reviews will ensure consistent performance. In this section, we will introduce a concept called Organizational tacking.

The fifth step is how we maintain our new state of our organization.

If we follow the process and achieve and commit to holding

Creating the Path of Organizational Change Timeline

each step on our path of change, we can begin to see the new state of our organization. Unaffected by our past, secure in our reality, arriving at choices that will help us maintain our stability, and constantly working toward ongoing development. This is our new state, as outlined in the illustration above.

The following chapters will provide deeper insights into each step.

CHAPTER 9

Our Existing State and the Effects of the Past

You can't go back and change the beginning,
but you can start where you are and change the ending.
—C. S. Lewis

The first step involves a review of leadership, employee engagement, and past processes in all areas of the operation. This allows us to question all the decisions that have taken place over the years to determine how we arrived at our current state. It is similar to establishing a baseline we use to measure improvements. When seeking to improve operations and processes within organizations, we must establish a baseline that will provide a starting point to gauge our success. Change for the sake of change is useless, and any organizational changes must be well thought out and provide measurable improvement.

Key areas of a review would, of course, include all operational results. Financial reviews include but are not limited to budgets, historical data on profit and losses, debt to equity, staffing requirements, etc. This review is standard, and the measurements will be compared with similar organizations within the industry. Having someone with a finance background would be helpful in the study. The financial review is an area that most organizations place a lot of weight on. Financial success and operating at budget are critical, but individuals within the organization drive them.

We will focus most of this chapter on an organization's soft skills, including the review of leadership, employee engagement, and process-centric systems. Each section will highlight the rower, sitter, and driller philosophy. Let's begin.

Leadership

How are organizations struggling to improve processes, create culture, provide quality output, and achieve overall success? In most cases, it is reflective of poor leadership.

Gallup has found that one of the most important decisions companies make is whom they name a manager. Yet our analytics suggest they usually get it wrong. Gallup finds that companies fail to choose the candidate with the right talent for the job 82 percent of the time. In one study of 7,272 US adults, Gallup found that 50 percent of employees left their job "to get away from their manager to improve their overall life at some point in their career."[19]

Poor leadership affects the ability of organizations to innovate, creating new processes, products, or services. One example is represented by managers who are drillers. Managers who are drillers are worried about how they appear to their bosses and will hide the truth of the condition within organizations. When the truth is discovered, they blame others for the uncovered issues. Drillers tend not to be process-centric because they work from a chaotic position. Chaos prevents others from seeing the actual condition of an organization. People working for drillers are in survival mode. Sitters will sit and attempt to follow the leaders' decisions. Rowers will struggle but eventually become frustrated and leave the organization. Drilling leaders will negotiate poor agreements since they struggle with building relationships. Organizations then must deal with the fallout of imperfect union or supplier contracts. They are experts at deflecting all blame to others. Process improvement through collaboration is nonexistent since they view their decisions as final.

Leaders who are sitters struggle with making decisions. They tend not to be proactive and may even have low conscientiousness. Due to these shortcomings, they struggle to move organizations in a process-centric direction. They tend to be the leaders who embrace the status quo. This makes leaders who are sitters past process-centric, meaning they like processes but may not seek to improve them. They will defend their actions and can

---

19. *State of the American Manager: Analytics and Advice for Leaders*, Gallup, 2015.

be lost in the system when operations run smoothly. When operations falter, however, their inability to lead becomes obvious. By then it is too late.

Leaders who are rowers create dynamic structures within the organization. They are very process-centric, viewing process improvement as opportunities for creating better outcomes. Rowers are positive leaders who utilize gain framing when dealing with issues and focus on positive results that can be mirrored to improve all areas of the operation. They are very collaborative, seeking buy-in from everyone to ensure that the process is supported and outcomes can be correctly measured. They empower their teams with the ongoing development of job skills and behaviors that endorse partnerships and success at every level. It is essential at this point to understand that leaders have inherent traits that make them good leaders, but they also need to be trained to manage as much as lead. Many believe they are two mutually exclusive tasks, but they are not. Although there is a technical difference in the outcome of both, they must be one and the same. Over the years of working in facilities, many used the excuse of not managing since they were leaders. And at times managers would use the reason of managing with fear based on the excuse that the leaders will provide the relationship building. When we separate the two, we notice that most want to defer to leading since it is considered the higher cause with less friction; however, they are two different styles. They should not be used as an excuse not to manage or lead.

During one of our consulting projects, we were brought into a large organization to provide management training. Through working with several managers who we had determined to be rowers, we uncovered a frustration they all were experiencing. They felt the department director used their leadership to force the managers to make tough decisions. During department meetings, the department head would speak of the vision and mission and provide good motivation to the staff. But would not offer support for the managers interpreting their role as only that of inspiration. The director would have a different approach during the manager's team meetings. They demanded action and insisted that they implement intimidating strategies to gain higher productivity.

When we approached the director with our observation, the leader responded that that was their interpretation of leadership to the department and managing the managers. The adjustment was simple, and since the director and the managers were rowers, the result was immediate. We explained that leaders are responsible for all outcomes and creating a safe environment for all levels of their responsibility. The fix was easy. During full staff meetings, the managers would provide, in a gain-framing process, examples of proper outcomes. The meeting was used to create a safe environment to share ideas and explore the successes within the department and how they could be mirrored in other areas to produce more success. By endorsing the successful outcomes, the director not only supported the managers in front of the staff but also motivated the managers and, in turn, produced strong loyalty. The staff, in turn, respected the manager's role since the director recognized and endorsed it.

There is a fine line between leading and managing. Great leaders are not afraid to manage when necessary and great managers know they must also lead. Rowers can adapt quickly to see the need for self-improvement, embrace the process, and apply the changes rapidly.

How do we find the managers who exhibit behaviors conducive to successful management? Gallup defines this as talent.

Gallup defines *talent* as the natural capacity for excellence. People can learn skills, develop knowledge and gain experience, but they cannot acquire talent—it is innate. Individuals with the right talent for their role think and act differently than their peers. They are energized by their work, rarely thinking of it as "work" at all. But for others whose talent is not the best fit, the same work can feel draining."

"Companies that hire managers based on talent realize a 48 percent increase in profitability, a 22 percent increase in productivity, a 30 percent increase in employee engagement scores, a 17 percent increase in customer engagement scores, and a 19 percent decrease in turnover."[20]

Gallup explains that talent cannot be detected in a resume or through most interview processes. Gallup and other organizations utilize assessments to determine innate characteristics and talent, which we refer to as personalities.

As we reviewed in our previous chapters, Rowers have particular personalities and exhibit key behaviors due to these personalities that make them successful. Primarily, they know how to engage the team.

---

20. *State of the American Manager: Analytics and Advice for Leaders*, Gallup, 2015.

Employee Engagement

Since the start of the Industrial Revolution, organizations have focused all their attention on raising productivity within their workforce. Longer workdays, longer workweeks, new technology, and other external means were utilized to increase production. When workers rebelled, they were terminated, and the worker's well-being to improve production or service was not an option. Unions were created to protect workers at the turn of the last century, but their involvement created a more significant separation of management and employees.

In recent years, we have realized that employee engagement is the key to increasing productivity and excellent service.

"In one of the largest studies of burnout, Gallup found the biggest source was 'unfair treatment at work.' That was followed by an unmanageable workload, unclear communication from managers, lack of manager support and unreasonable time pressure. Those five causes have one thing in common: your boss. Get a bad one and you are almost guaranteed to hate your job. A bad boss will ignore you, disrespect you and never support you. Environments like that can make anyone miserable. A manager's effect on a workplace is so significant that Gallup can predict 70 percent of the variance in team engagement just by getting to know the boss."

"When employees are engaged and thriving, they experience significantly less stress, anger, and health problems. Nevertheless, globally, only 9 percent of employees are in that thriving and engaged category—while the majority (57 percent) of the world's employees are not engaged and not thriving."[21]

Our company, HHA Services, managed contract services for service departments in medical centers throughout the United States. In over 90 percent of the facilities we contracted to service, the management of the departments was the biggest issue. Once replaced, and we had implemented an employee engagement process, the staff would flourish, and our third-party quality scores would increase.

Reviewing work schedules, start and stop times, workloads, and equipment needs is the beginning of creating an engaged workforce. Utilizing employee engagement surveys is the best way to review the current relationship between the staff and management. Employee well-being initiatives should include but not be limited to examining benefits that improve physical and mental health. Examples include standing desks, healthy snacks, wellness information, discounts for gym memberships, flexible schedules, and other wellness programs. Meetings should be designed to provide positive feedback and celebrations of excellent service. Establishing changes in the department or facility should be a shared review, allowing the staff to contribute to the potential changes.

At one location in a large Midwest medical center, our company was brought in to provide management of their environmental services department. The medical center had just added a new wing to the facility, and they were hoping through our experience, we would not only raise the quality of the services but maintain existing staffing levels, including the addition of

---

21. *State of the Global Workforce 2022 Report*, Gallup, 2022.

the new wing. The establishment of employee engagement processes and a change in the management not only increased the quality of services we held to the existing staffing when the new wing opened. This occurred with a rise in employee job satisfaction measured by a third-party survey.

Rowers are excited about implementing employee engagement initiatives. They understand the importance of an engaged workforce, and all surveys we reviewed showed engaged managers produced engaged workforces. The statics prove that organizations need engaged rowers to succeed in engaging the workforce.

"It should come as no surprise that managers have the greatest impact on employee engagement. Managers are responsible for setting job expectations, providing constructive feedback, encouraging growth and development, and building strong teams. Managers who do these tasks well inspire employees to perform at their best, while managers who fumble at these tasks spur employees to look for new jobs."[22]

Process-Centric Operation

The final review involves the processes in place that produce the business outcomes. Although we included the concept of process-centric in the leadership section above, we added this section to explain further. Process-centric organizations divide all

22. *State of the American Manager: Analytics and Advice for Leaders*, Gallup, 2015.

tasks into smaller procedures to develop specific improvements at all phases. Process improvements can only occur if we have established processes to track and measure.

Within our service departments at our medical centers, having established cleaning procedures for all isolation rooms was critical in both the consistent execution of the procedures and the ability to measure the success of the results based on the incidence of cross-contamination of another room. Or within our food service division, the quality of the recipe and final meal could only be measured based on a review of proper procedures during meal preparation.

The BPM Institute defines a process-centric organization as the following:[23]

1. **Define realistic and clear goals**

   In a process-centric organization, defining your target goal is essential to getting desired results. Defining realistic and clear goals ultimately helps organizations to focus on the right priorities, and progress helps employees stay motivated to drive the right outcomes.

   » Why do we need to define realistic and clear goals?
     It is because clear goals are target oriented and easy to understand. Realistic goals can be achieved with a proper strategy. We must be able to define goals and targets as per an employee's capability.

---

23. Bergs, Anthony. "5 Steps to Creating a Process-Centric Organization Without Losing Human Touch!" BPM Institute.

This way, he performs the best to get the efficient results.

2. **Scale expectations with reality**

Always check if your employees fit into your organizations. Do best-fit hiring of the employees so that they merge well in your work environment and culture. Give achievable targets to them so they can achieve them and stay motivated. Scale your expectations with reality—that is, know the potential qualities and scope of improvement in your workforce!

3. **For new employees, the learning curve matters**

In a company, every department is interconnected. They have to work in sync to achieve the targets. Hence, whenever hiring a new employee, give them proper time for training for the processes of the organization and understanding peer-to-peer relationship building. This way it will be easier for the employees to blend into the culture of your process-centric organization.

4. **Mix-and-match: Innovation + Efficiency**

Every process-centric organization aims at achieving effective results. The organizations must look for employees who are innovative and efficient enough to achieve the desired results. Hire those people who can;

» Take the initiative and have an enterprising nature.
» Develop ideas and create solutions on their own.
» They must be confident enough in getting the work done rightly!

They must be productive, and they must respect deadlines and submit their assignments well on time so that it doesn't hamper the company's reputation in the market. They must also know the importance of achieving the ultimate organizational goals.

5. **Maintain a work-life balance**

Usually, product-centric companies have more workload of finishing their targets well on time with the best quality. Maintain a better work- life balance in your organization to maintain a good retention rate. When we talk about work-life balance, it's never about adding more work to the mix, but always about adding more life.

During the process review stage, we can understand the operation of an organization before making changes that may have been a part of the organization's original process but may have changed due to management not following up a lack of proper training, or a misunderstanding of the process itself.

Summary

Step one of creating the path of organizational change involved a review of leadership and management, employee engagement, and process-centric operations. Each area influences the ability to develop a successful operation moving through our timeline. And we can see through the references, statistics, and examples the influence rowers in management and leadership positions have on the organization's success.

CHAPTER 10

Evaluating the Current Reality

*The enterprise that does not innovate ages
and declines, and in a period of rapid change,
such as the present, the decline will be fast.*
—Peter Drucker

T he donkey said to the tiger: "The grass is blue."

The tiger replied: "No, the grass is green."

The discussion heated up, and the two decided to submit to arbitration, and for this, they went before the lion, the king of the jungle.

Already before reaching the forest clearing, where the lion was sitting on his throne, the donkey began to shout: "His Highness, is it true that the grass is blue?"

The lion replied: "True, the grass is blue."

The donkey hurriedly continued: "The tiger disagrees with me and contradicts and annoys me. Please punish him."

The king then declared: "The tiger will be punished with five years of silence."

The donkey jumped cheerfully and went on his way, content and repeating: "The grass is blue."

The tiger accepted his punishment, but before doing so he asked the lion: "Your Majesty, why have you punished me? After all, the grass is green."

The lion replied: "In fact, the grass is green."

The tiger asked: "So why are you punishing me?"

The lion replied: "That has nothing to do with the question of whether the grass is blue or green. The punishment is because it is not possible for a brave and intelligent creature like you to waste time arguing with a donkey, and on top of that, come and bother me with that question."

The worst waste of time is arguing with the fool and fanatic who does not care about truth or reality but only the victory of his beliefs and illusions. Never waste time on arguments that don't make sense . . . There are people who, no matter how much evidence we present to them, are not in the capacity to understand, and others are blinded by ego, hatred and resentment, and all they want is to be right even if they are not. When ignorance screams, intelligence is silent. Your peace and quiet are worth more.

I use this parable of the donkey and the tiger to elicit the inner question in each of us: What is our reality, and are we willing to accept our actual reality? Are we like the donkey who sees the grass as blue and refuses to accept what is true? Or are we like the tiger wasting time debating what is true?

Either way, when organizations don't evaluate their current condition, understand what is actual, and establish processes based on the actual, they are doomed to fail. This chapter will assess the actions necessary for organizational transformation, including why it is difficult for individuals to lead change. Then we will utilize the SWOT[24] analysis and other tools to determine our current reality in preparation for the potential change that will need to take place.

Since we will rely on leaders to evaluate the current reality and begin the change process, we must first identify why individuals struggle with change. Our struggle to accept what can happen to us in our lives can be explained through science. In a study by the University of Hertfordshire published on March 7, 2014, *Self-Acceptance Could Be the Key to a Happier Life. Yet, It's the Happy Habit Many People Practice the Least*, a survey of five thousand people rated themselves between 1 and 10 on the ten habits that identified the latest scientific research as the keys to happiness and most closely related to people's overall satisfaction with life. Acceptance is the strongest habit that predicts people's happiness and satisfaction with life. Yet acceptance was also revealed as the habit that people practice the least, generating the lowest average score from the five thousand respondents.

Regarding the acceptance question, the study's results from the respondents were as follows: How often are you kind to yourself

---

24. Humphrey, Albert. "Strength, Weaknesses, Opportunity, and Threats." Stanford Research Institute, 1960.

and think you're fine as you are? The average rating was just 5.56 out of 10. Only 5 percent of people put themselves at a 10 on the acceptance habit. Around one in five people (19 percent) scored an 8 or 9; less than one-third (30 percent) scored a 6 or 7; and almost half (46 percent) of people rated themselves at 5 or less.

If we cannot accept ourselves for who we are, we will certainly not be able to lead change within an organization.

So why do we struggle so much with being with what is and accepting who we are? The answer is in our ancestry and evolution from the caves to our modern world. It is a form of survival from prehistoric times, rooted deep in the structure of our brains. As we discussed in previous chapters, genetics plays a factor in how we respond to almost every situation we face in our lifetime. The effort to break out of what our genetic composition has given us is complex and can be overwhelming.

In an article published in the *Harvard Business Review*, Professor Rosabeth Moss Kanter identifies ten reasons leaders resist change. Loss of control over the leader's territory, excess uncertainty in whether the change will work, decisions imposed on people suddenly, being creatures of habit, we choose the routine, loss of face if it doesn't work, our concerns of competency of being able to make the change work, change is more work. Change creates disruption in other areas, past resentments of changes that didn't work, and the idea that the change may eliminate positions. "Leadership is about change, but what can a leader do when faced with ubiquitous resistance? Resistance to change manifests in many ways, from foot-dragging and inertia to petty sabotage and outright rebellions. The best tool for leaders of change is to understand the predictable, universal sources of resistance in each situation and then strategize around them."[25]

Understanding why change is so challenging to implement within organizations is critical as we begin evaluating the organization's current reality. Leaders set the stage for change, and organizational transformation will not occur when leaders responsible for the change are unwilling or incapable of leading the transformation.

Let's begin with the tools that can help the transformation to occur in an organized format. Then we will review the effects of the rower, sitter, and driller in the transformation process.

SWOT analysis is an excellent tool we have utilized to transform many companies over the past thirty years. The SWOT analysis provides a review of all operational processes and an opportunity to reestablish the mission and vision of the organization. The process is simple; utilizing teams from all divisions of the organization in a collaborative format, each lists out what they believe to be the strengths, weaknesses, opportunities, and threats. Strengths and weaknesses are considered internal, and opportunities and threats are external. Once each division or section is completed, there is an opportunity to review responses to eliminate duplication and develop a company-wide list for each SWOT. The team then divides the list by areas of responsibility. Keeping in mind some responses may require two departments to work together. We also advise separating the list by priorities based on easy to accomplish up to difficult or costly. Goals and time commitments are established and reported each month.

25. Kanter, Rosabeth Moss. "Ten Reasons People Resist Change." *Harvard Business Review*, September 25, 2012.

There are many ways to go through the SWOT process and set goals specific to each response. We recommend that the process is collaborative and that the result is goals are established and followed up regularly.

The following are examples of a SWOT analysis:

Strengths: What an organization sees as its internal strengths that set it apart from all other organizations. Strengths include but are not limited to proprietary tools; service marked and unique processes, brand strength and awareness, and development programs.

A great example would be the strength of a brand name like Coke. Another example is at our company, HHA Services; we developed Q-School as a three-day development course for new leaders, managers, and supervisors. These are examples of strengths that other organizations may not have, or if they did, they wouldn't be as strong.

Weaknesses: An organization sees weaknesses as internal issues that limit its competitiveness with other companies. Weaknesses include but are not limited to staffing issues such as expertise in an important function, a slow hiring process, or the lack of an established orientation program.

At our company ELM Learning, we redesigned our hiring and orientation process. Reviewing the assessments, interviews, and background checks took too long. Then, once hired, the orientation process was too long and not specific to the needs of each division. Surveys indicated this was a weakness, so we created a more streamlined hiring and orientation process.

Opportunities: Opportunities are external to the organization. They can include but are not limited to a new product line, a new technology that can be integrated into our process to make it more efficient, or a new service line.

An example of an opportunity would be adding breakfast to the services offered by a local restaurant and creating a new product that will provide additional income to an organization. Tesla created the first complete line of electric-powered automobiles, and soon after, Ford Motor Company created a new line of electric-powered vehicles. In 2001 HHA established our food services division, creating a new revenue stream and making our company a stronger contender in larger medical centers.

Threats: Threats represent external factors that can influence the success of an organization. These include but are not limited to government regulatory decisions, changes in the industry due to the economy, and global crises.

An example of a threat would be a global pandemic or a goods and services tax increase. During the COVID-19 pandemic, most businesses were forced to close. Our video company could not get access to the medical centers to shoot necessary training and video. Our digital learning company has maintained and increased business due to corporations' need for online training. We closed our physical offices in New York and San Diego, forcing our support services team to work at providing supplies and equipment to our teams who now work from home.

Other tools and processes for transformation include the following:

1. SOAR analysis maintains the strength and opportunities but offers aspirations and results. Aspirations focus on the organizational desires, including who and where

they will serve and operate, and the results address how they will accomplish and track the progress of the aspirations and opportunities. Designed to help startup companies.

2. NOISE analysis is divided into Needs, Opportunities, Improvements, Strengths, and Exceptions and framed as an analysis based on what you don't have instead of what you need to overcome from a SWOT analysis.

There are more, but these are all reasonably similar in that they are tools for organizational analysis.

Let's spend some time analyzing how rowers, sitters, and drillers respond to the current reality and the need to initiate organizational change as outlined in this chapter.

Drillers struggle with evaluating the current condition of an organization, and they see the process as a weakness and a challenge to their ego. And as we have learned in previous chapters, drillers resist changes that affect them directly or indirectly due to their egotistical nature. During the analysis, they will question the process and responses and create disorder. The disorder is a diversion, taking the focus initially away from them. Then they will step in with a solution that fits their needs and appear as the hero of the situation. They will also blame others who may be close to them or involved in any way, never owning up to what they should accept as their need for change. They expect any necessary change to come from the world around them. It is difficult for people in relationships with drillers to accept what is happening in their life since the driller constantly controls them.

Sitters will default that if it isn't broken, why are we fixing it, fearful of what change may be necessary to take place? They can become frozen in accepting the current state, even giving up. The NeuroLeadership Institute published a study in 2019 that provided research on how change impacts our brains. The results indicate that our brains have evolved from our basic desire to survive and to prefer certainty. Evolution has optimized our ability to live by predicting and controlling our circumstances. When faced with change, our brains can either interpret the change as a threat or a challenge. When perceived as a threat, this leads to emotional stress. We also experience distress physiologically. These responses include but are not limited to shortness of breath, elevated heart rate, and restricted blood flow. These effects can make us feel that change is impossible based on the limits of our capacity to cope. We become stuck in our current situation, with no chance of producing a satisfactory solution. We cannot accept what is beyond what we have already interpreted as our reality, which has allowed us to survive within our established boundaries of safety created by our past. So we sit.

Let's focus on what contributes to our ability to be a rower. According to the study on self-acceptance, when we experience change as a challenge, we see the opportunity to learn or do something different. We experience the opposite of distress or eustress because the new demands of the change seem within our abilities. The study explains: "During eustress, our bodies also respond efficiently. Our hearts still beat faster, but now with a decrease in vascular resistance, meaning blood can flow throughout the circulatory system with greater ease. We either feel more positive or, at the very least, less bad in the face of the change we are experiencing."[26]

Rowers naturally rise to meet the needs of the organization. They can accept the necessary changes viewing the potential changes as new challenges and opportunities.

Our company had decided to form a marketing relationship with another health-care services company in the late 1990s. We had agreed to bring in a local university professor to oversee the transition and aid us in the strategic review. Our company had also decided to conduct a SWOT, and we were excited to get the entire involved in the process. Immediately it became apparent who were the rowers, sitters, and drillers. The rowers provided concrete responses throughout the SWOT process. They became physically excited and offered suggestions with enthusiasm. They became a part of the process, taking notes and huddling with other rowers to create collaboration. They were change champions.

The sitters were quiet during the process. At times they would offer ideas and suggestions because of the attention the rowers were getting, but they could not lead the change. They, at times, would ask questions seeking clarification, but mostly they were willing to sit and see what unfolded. Rowers would identify the sitters and seek their collaboration and approval of their ideas. When left alone, sitters preferred to sit; when necessary, if the room was full of energy and the rowers were rowing, they would support the changes.

---

26. Derler, Andrea, and Ray, Jennifer. "Why Change is so Hard—and How to Deal with It." NeuroLeadership Institute, December 12, 2019.

Drillers were very active during the process. Sometimes suggested that there was no need to seek out ideas, and at times creating confusion by analyzing the suggestions as they were being offered. One of the critical processes in a SWOT is that there are no bad suggestions or ideas. Everyone has a voice, and no one would be judged, and drillers judged. They attacked when they saw weakness in the individual causing the individual to sit. The sitters didn't want to get embarrassed and would stop rowing, and the rowers would become frustrated. In this case, drillers do not seek collaboration. They seek chaos. From the ruins of confusion, the driller provides their solution to fix the issue and then enjoys the opportunity to be the hero.

We powered through the SWOT by establishing rules of engagement. Hands would have to be raised to offer suggestions, and when choosing the final essential recommendations for future goals, we did it in a ballot format. Thereby taking the voice away from the drillers and allowing the sitters to have a voice.

When we finalized our SWOT and established the goals for the next two years, we presented them to the professor. He was impressed that we utilized a successful process before we even knew and created the concept of rowers, sitters, and drillers. He said that the SWOT process also allowed us to see who would help champion the company into the future. And we would also have witnessed through the process who would have to find a new job. He understood the effect of rowers and drillers on an organization.

CHAPTER 11

Implementing Change

It is not necessary to change; survival isn't necessary.
—W. Edwards Deming

Once we have completed our strategic analysis utilizing our tool of choice, such as the SWOT analysis outlined in the previous chapter, we will begin implementing the collaborated changes. This chapter is dedicated to the change process. In most organizations, the implementation of change falls short of what was arrived at in the analysis. Many models cite the difficulty in successfully implementing change, such as Kotter's 8-Step Process and Lewin's Change Management Model are two of the more popular models. Kotter advises creating the urgency of the need for change, utilizing strong leaders who can implement the change. The process also suggests building the vision and providing strong communication to gain momentum. Finally, remove all obstacles and create quick wins.

Lewin's Change Management Model creates the perception of the need for change within the organization. Then establishing the appropriate behaviors to accomplish the transformation and, finally, establishing the new behavior as the norm.

The change models all provide a process that includes a collaborative process, strong leadership, and the need for behavior modification at the individual and organizational levels. Behavior modification at a personal level is a complex but necessary process to accomplish organizational changes and meet goals promptly and positively successfully. Change, however, is not a natural part of our brain's function, as we discovered in the previous chapter. Motivation is a driving force to help employees accept and support change; however, we cannot motivate only when we need support for change. Excellent leaders always motivate. The National Leader Institute identified five domains in the human social experience, the SCARF® Model.[27]

They include Status, the need for employees to stand out from the crowd. Certainty, the need to understand their responsibilities and roles related to the organization, no surprises. Autonomy is a sense of control over their work and decisions to accomplish it—relatedness or the sense of belonging. Good leaders endorse this with formal language such as we instead of me. Fairness is identified as a sense of equity and equality. They are communicating not only the change or the goal to be achieved

---

27. "5 Ways to Spark (or Destroy) Your Employees' Motivation." NeuroLeadership Institute, September13, 2022.

but also the thought process of how the change or the goal is arrived at.

Rowers endorse the SCARF® Model in the day-to-day management of their team. This allows them to establish trust and instill meaning in their employees without feeling threatened. Drillers struggle with sharing information and tend to micro-manage their employees. Their chaotic management style does not provide certainty. They attempt to push change through, sometimes using intimidating strategies to accomplish their goals. Sitters struggle with utilizing the methods in the SCARF® Model. They can rise to the occasion if rowers on their team support them; however, they can become quiet and even remove themselves from engagement in the change process if drillers challenge them. Proper leadership is critical in the successful outcome of accomplishing any change or meeting any goals within an organization.

The initial step has been accomplished by utilizing a collaborative effort to arrive at the changes that need to occur. Using a collaborative approach helps to get buy-in from everyone involved. Where the process falls short in most organizations is at the implementation. Consider that the organization's leaders work jointly with the managers and critical personnel to develop the SWOT analysis and establish the agreed-upon changes. Most leaders who can lead through the process correctly tend to be rowers. Then they turn over the implementation to managers and team leaders responsible for the performance. The mistake companies make in this step is they place highly skilled managers in charge of the process without considering whether they are rowers, sitters, and drillers. We have seen it repeatedly at many facilities where certain leaders' outcomes are more productive than others. In some cases, the manager or lead is a sitter struggling to meet the goals because, in the past, they have not dealt with the drillers that now influence their team. Or the manager who is a driller has created a toxic environment where rowers have left for another part of the organization or another company.

Rowers define the need for change by communicating the current state and the change process and providing the advantage for the change. This is positive or gain framing. Drillers tell what needs to be accomplished and what will happen if it is not completed. This is an example of negative or loss framing.

Each change should be in a format that provides the employee with clear reasons and outcomes. Keep it simple, not more than one or two sentences. Too much information is not necessary for the organization to accept the change. But be prepared to answer questions and provide more detail upon request.

At one of our SWOT processes, we identified a weakness in properly utilizing protective garments in our isolation rooms. It was unanimously decided that we should create a new video with supporting documentation for the training process. The programs were completed and sent out to the facilities. Each facility was responsible for conducting the new training and providing proper documentation to show each trainee's competency. And at each facility, the managers would assign their supervisors and leaders to complete the training on each shift. The flow from the leaders who worked with teams to develop the training and the actual trainers involved four levels. The results provided an opportunity to measure our leadership teams at each facility. We realized that the highly engaged, energetic leaders, managers, and trainers accomplished the training and fulfilled the competency requirements of each trainee. These represented our rowers; they created enthusiasm with their teams. Some made a gamified process; others created videos of the bloopers. They had already established trust with their teams, so the training was easy to accept, and they felt a deep desire to perform for the leaders at their facility.

The drillers were, in most cases, able to succeed in accomplishing all the training, but the results were very different. The trainees felt a sense of requirement to complete the training. They cooperated out of fear, and with that, their competency was minimal. Drillers focus on fear and intimidating strategies to accomplish goals. They struggle with participation with others and prefer to command rather than to ask. When we visited the locations, we noticed no consistent process outlined in the training for them to utilize the protective garments. When questioned, some employees admitted forgetting the process but were afraid to ask.

The sitters were also able to finish the training at their facilities; however, their timelines were the longest. They required constant follow-up to ensure the training was scheduled and completed. When questioned, they always provided reasons for the delay. And in most organizations, since they would not be recognized as sitters, it would be accepted. Sitters are not as proactive as rowers, and they may delay the outcome or become affected by drillers on the team. They also struggle with conscientiousness, paying close attention to the detail. Although they tend to be success-focused most of the time, they fail in most cases to deliver desired results.

Another critical step is developing an achievable timeline. It should include phases of the change to get to the result. We like to utilize the sailing term *tacking* when we make organizational changes. Essential adjustments are constantly made with the sails to keep the boat moving optimally. Adjustments or tacking occur when the wind or the waves change, affecting the boat's efficiency. Organizational tacking, as we define it, is small changes over periods allowing for adjustments based on the responses received during the process. In the case of the new training program for protective clothing, there were many phases to consider in the project's overall success. Script writing, video production, editing, and final review are involved in just the video production. From there, the video needed to be tested at a location that could provide honest feedback to ensure the accuracy of the training video. Most organizations have key managers they trust to provide credible feedback (rowers!). If adjustments must be made to the training, then there needs to be a change in the timeline.

Finally, the packaging and communication to the facilities must be clear. The communication must clearly explain the original training process and what was missing, resulting in the need for change. The change process should be communicated to include all the individuals who were involved in the process. Next, the communication should consist of the new video's positive attributes that will help add credibility to the change—also citing the increase in safety and the welfare of the staff by providing this new training. Finally, the closing should be exciting, creating momentum and praising the anticipated cooperation.

All these steps are just in releasing the new training videos and process. There will be timelines at each facility dealing with scheduling issues, absenteeism, and training room availability, to name just a few. And although the overall organization timeline may be one year for all facilities to roll out the change, there must be flexibility based on issues that will naturally occur. Utilizing organizational tacking will help leaders realize that matters beyond their control can hinder meeting deadlines.

The final step in our implementing change process is the recognition and celebration of small and big wins. Nothing motivates people like recognition and gratitude. Focusing on "low-hanging fruit" helps provide momentum in the change process. This means creating wins by solving easy issues before tackling the most challenging problems. This will also allow you to be sure you have rowers leading the change. Rowers utilize sincere gratitude and appreciation and can instill meaning in recognition of the work of team members. Rowers can provide appreciation and gratefulness to team members since they have high emotional intelligence, are open to other perspectives, and are conscientious. One of many studies on personalities and gratitude cites, "The results showed that both gratitude and emotional intelligence correlated positively and significantly with extraversion, openness to experience, agreeableness, and conscientiousness."[28] As our studies have indicated, rowers have inherent personality traits that allow them to naturally express gratitude, praise, and appreciation to others who perform at expected or higher standards.

---

28. Szcześniak, Malgorzata, Rodzeń, Wojciech, Malinowska, Angieszka, and Kroplewski, Zdzisiaw. "The Big Five Personality Traits and Gratitude: The Role of Emotional Intelligence." *Psychology Research and Behavior Management* 13 (November 11, 2020): 977–988. doi: 10.2147/PRBM.S268643.

As outlined in the previous chapter, drillers tend to be ego-centric, which is not conducive to expressing gratitude. They crave personal praise and blame others when issues occur, or timelines are unmet. "Our genes and our brains aren't the end of the story; certain personality factors can also act as barriers to gratitude. In particular, envy, materialism, narcissism, and cynicism can be thought of as thieves of thankfulness."[29] Don't be mistaken—drillers can and will accomplish tasks through others. The difference is, they command respect and don't earn respect from their teams. As witnessed in our protective equipment training process, the results were different in both the outcome based on the skills of the trainees and the culture established at the rower, sitter, and driller locations.

---

29. Allen, Summer. "Why Is Gratitude So Hard for Some People?" *Greater Good Magazine*. May 10, 2018.

CHAPTER 12

Developing Consistent Performance

You cannot consistently perform in a manner
which is inconsistent with the way you see yourself.
—Zig Ziglar

W hy is consistency so important in leading and managing people? Consistent leaders are emotionally stable, providing a balanced approach to issues that may occur during the workday. They communicate with their employees often, providing positive feedback and utilizing gain framing to correct issues. They maintain a consistent yet flexible approach when focusing on the goals. They constantly encourage creativity by providing an open-door policy. Leaders who offer this level of consistency have very loyal employees. The employees know they can trust their leader.

Having worked with and developed many supervisors, managers, and leaders over the past thirty years, we have connected consistency with the energy expended by the individual. In an article published in *Forbes Magazine*, "15 Things Effective Leaders Do With Extreme Consistency," by Brent Gleeson, June 15, 2020, he points out that influential leaders consistently strive with extreme discipline. They form consistent behaviors and apply the energy necessary to achieve success. We see this type of leader in the actions of rowers. Consistent leadership develops consistent performance. It is a top-down process.

The opposite of a consistent manager is an inconsistent manager. "In general, these people seemed to be perceived as not caring about outcomes at work and lazy about their job in general. A little inconsistency appeared to have a profoundly negative effect on almost every other competency and behavior."[30] The article explains inconsistent managers were not trusted to make decisions or trusted by their team members. They did not follow up on objectives and could be distracted. Failed to achieve goals, resisted self-improvement, did not have a cooperative nature, and could not anticipate problems until it was too late.

Inconsistency in leaders has been attributed to individual laziness. Laziness can be linked to many negative traits we must avoid continuing on the path of organizational and personal change. It can hinder our growth and the establishment of

---

30. Folkman, Joseph. "Your Inconsistency Is More Noticeable Than You Think." *Forbes Magazine*, October 17, 2019.

successful relations. It causes individuals to miss opportunities that could be impactful at other jobs and in their life.

Through our experience, sitters can be construed as being inconsistent and therefore lazy in the performance of their jobs. As read further, laziness is a biological condition. Laziness is a condition that can be modified through recognition and effort. This holds in our experience of witnessing sitters becoming rowers. First, let's understand what occurs in our brains.

In an article by Scott Jeffrey, published on Psych Central on April 10, 2017, he suggested that certain voices and expressions influence our behaviors that cause laziness in most people:

- Confusion: "I don't know what to do." This could be a temporary state that will pass with focus.
- Neurotic fear: "I just can't." Instead of the fight-or-flight response, we just freeze. The only way out is to face the fear.
- Fixed mindset: "I'm afraid I'll fail or look stupid." With a fixed mindset, people fear trying new things because they want to look smart and talented, even though they lack experience. In contrast, individuals with a growth mindset know their talents, abilities, and intelligence can develop through deliberate effort and practice.
- Lethargy: "I'm too tired." We invest a lot of energy suppressing our lazy side. The more we run from it, the stronger it becomes in our unconscious. When you feel lethargic, instead of stimulating yourself with caffeine, accept your fatigue.
- Apathy: "I just don't care about anything." Apathy is

the voice of depression. Sometimes we live off our true course, doing too many things we don't like. We confuse disinterest with laziness.

- Regret: "I'm too old to get started." Regret only holds us back when we don't allow ourselves to grieve the past. These voices are just beliefs, not truths. They are excuses not to get started *right now*.
- Identity: "I'm just a lazy person." When we hear this voice, it's a sure sign our lazy side has hijacked us. When we're centered, we are neutral. We don't define ourselves as either lazy people or the opposite (achievers). We just are.

An article titled "Laziness Is Not a Trait," published on April 7, 2021, on Symptoms of Living, confirms laziness is not associated with personality traits. The article explains laziness is a habit that can be broken. It cites similar influences as the article above and provides us with actions that need to take place to change our lazy habits. They include breaking down tasks so they are manageable and less intimidating and finding knowledge and learning to fill the gaps that may hinder you from moving forward with a project. When you lack the motivation, ask questions and try visualizing what the end product will look like.

Other research suggests that although laziness is not a personality trait, it can be tied to certain chemicals in our brain, and where those chemicals reside can determine our laziness.

Psychologists believe laziness reflects a lack of self-esteem or a lack of positive recognition by others. They identify that a lack of discipline stemming from low self-confidence, a lack of interest in the activity, or belief in its need, may create laziness. Motivation studies have shown that overstimulation, excessive impulses, or distractions can cause laziness. These, in turn, increase the release of a dopamine neurotransmitter responsible for reward and pleasure. The more dopamine released, the greater the intolerance for valuing and accepting productive and rewarding actions. This desensitization leads to dulling of the neural patterns and can negatively affect the part of the brain responsible for risk perception, known as the anterior insula.

In another study cowritten by psychologist Michael Treadway from Vanderbilt University, Jennifer Welsh published the research and findings in the *Journal of Neurosciences*, updated on January 19, 2022, in Live Science.

Using brain scans of individuals considered to be "go-getters" and those identified as "slackers," there were differences in three parts of their brains. The chemical dopamine, linked to its influence on motivation and the feeling of reward when something has been accomplished, was identified in different brain regions for the go-getters and the slackers. The go-getters had more dopamine in the brain's striatum and ventromedial prefrontal cortex. Slackers had higher dopamine levels in an area of the brain called the anterior insula. This part of the brain is involved with emotions and risk perceptions. The study shows that dopamine can have opposite effects in different parts of the brain. In summary, their research suggests that more dopamine in the anterior insula area of the brain causes a reduced desire to work, even if money is offered as a reward. In the past, dopamine has always been considered to enhance reward-driven behavior.

The study above indicates that the release of dopamine in some regions of the brain can determine whether a person has a propensity to be more apathetic. "If it takes more energy to plan an action, it becomes more costly for apathetic people to make actions," explained one member of the study team, neurology researcher Masud Husain at the University of Oxford. "Their brains have to make more effort."[31]

Whether laziness is caused by voices or expressions that influence our behaviors or chemicals manufactured in our brain that could be located in specific areas impacting our laziness, we can agree that it will take more energy, preparation, and self-determination to bring a change and motivation sitters to move beyond sitting to become rowers.

Drillers thrive on inconsistent behavior as it relates to performance. Drillers can survive in most organizations where the leaders are focused on the task being accomplished and are not concerned with the process. Their behavior can be erratic, and their communications abrupt. Drillers believe that power over individuals is based on withholding information and through intimidating strategies. They create an environment of need. The employees rely on the driller to let them know what needs to be done. They begin to believe they must depend on the highly skilled driller to be successful and that ego-driven leaders must be good leaders. "Our research shows that the opposite seems

---

31. Bonnelle, Valerie, Manohar, Sanjay, Behrens, Tim, and Husain, Masud. "Individual Differences in Premotor Brain Systems Underlie Behavioral Apathy." *Cerebral Cortex* 26, 2 (February 2016): 807-819. doi: 10.1093/cercor/bhv247.

to be true,"[32] says Barbora Nevicka, a PhD candidate in organizational psychology, describing a new study she undertook with the University of Amsterdam colleagues Femke Ten Velden, Annebel De Hoogh and Annelies Van Vianen. The study found that narcissists' preoccupation with their brilliance inhibits a crucial element of successful group decision-making and performance: the free and creative exchange of information and ideas.

Many tools help provide consistent performance within organizations. We will review the tools we have found successful within our organizations and when we work with the companies we consult.

One-on-ones provide a consistent performance review on a regularly scheduled basis. We plan our one-on-one every two weeks at a scheduled time for each critical personnel. Monthly schedules for employees who have set work routines. Each organization can establish what works best. The key is constant communication, where issues can be addressed before they become significant problems, and positive feedback is provided to endorse positive outcomes. The meeting should be held privately with a set agenda that includes a review of the previous meeting's agenda, including outlined achievements. Provide open-ended questions and allow the employee to talk as much as possible. This is an opportunity for the employee to provide feedback relating to their work. Look for issues and opportunities that create work and personal development goals. Most one on ones take

32. Association for Psychological Science. "Narcissists Look Like Good Leaders—But They Aren't!" August 9, 2011. Accessed January 24, 2024. https://www.psychologicalscience.org/news/releases/narcissists-look-like-good-leadersbut-they-arent.html.

forty-five to sixty mins and should be kept in a written format. Focus on the conversation at hand. Turn off all devices and keep the meeting focused on the topics. Make sure the session ends on a high note. Show sincere gratefulness for their contribution and time in the meeting. One-on-ones are designed to take place or augment the annual review. In most organizations, we have eliminated the annual evaluation by utilizing one-on-ones.

Check-ins are different from one-on-ones in that they are informal and do not require documentation. They are also swift and should not interfere with the work routine. Check-in involves an opportunity to ask questions that relate to the individual's interests but are not of a personal nature that would make them feel uncomfortable. With remote workers, the importance of check-ins is magnified. They may also have to be scheduled; a video conference tool would be necessary. They are meant to be light and not an opportunity to discuss work performance.

Communication tools are essential in this time of remote workers. Tools that allow direct messaging, video formats, document sharing, and huddles keep the employees connected and provide open communications and sharing of ideas like an office environment.

Meetings remain essential to communicate and establish a connectedness with everyone. Brick-and-mortar organizations should set time aside for meetings to announce new processes and celebrate holidays, birthdays, anniversaries, and successful accomplishments. They can be scheduled regularly, allowing employees to plan their schedules.

Virtual meetings are equally essential to provide an opportunity for the teams to meet regularly.

The key to a successful meeting is to keep all discussions positive. It is an opportunity to create a culture of trust. Show gratefulness for what the employees have accomplished. Meetings that review negative issues involving a small group of those attending negatively impact the entire meeting. This is where rowers excel. They utilize the time together to pump up employees. They create energy and excitement. They joke and provide an atmosphere of caring. Drillers use the meetings as an opportunity to point out what everyone is doing wrong and what improvements need to take place and create an atmosphere of fear.

Studies have shown that positive meetings produce happier, more balanced workers and increase productivity by over 30 percent.

"New research from the fields of positive psychology and neuroscience shows that small shifts in the way we communicate can create big ripple effects on business outcomes, including 31 percent higher productivity, 25 percent greater performance ratings, 37 percent higher sales, and 23 percent lower levels of stress. Using scientifically supported communication strategies to extend a positive mindset can increase happiness and success at work for others as well as for ourselves, instantly making us more effective leaders."[33] The article explains the concept of the "power lead," that meetings should focus on accomplishments, provide an upbeat topic, highlight positive resources, inspire hope of a brighter future, and show gratitude.

---

33. "Five Minutes to Great Meetings: Start with the 'Power Lead,'" Wharton Executive Education, March 2018.

De-hassles help create a collaborative decision-making process. As we work through the SWOT analysis and the implementation of change from the analysis, we will face decisions along the way. A predetermined decision-making process will aid in consistently providing a fair and collaborative process. We have always used the de-hassle process as our decision-making tool. In this process, we identify all the stakeholders who need to be a part of the decision. Each person gets an opportunity to identify the issues that influence their success within a project or the organization. All items, like the SWOT analysis, are accepted, and no problem is excluded. Once all issues are on the list, it is then forced ranked to determine the priorities of the issues. Matters determined to be top priorities are established as goals that need to be resolved by a team or an individual. Deciding what is essential and what is not necessary is valuable since it is established through consensus. This allows rowers, sitters, and drillers an equal voice. The team then jointly establishes the yes and no of what must be resolved.

Once the decisions are made and the process completed, the next step is the proper communication of the change in a clear and concise format. Providing information to everyone is vital in the execution of the process. Receiving feedback is critical in identifying issues before they become insurmountable. Organizations with remote workers throughout the region, country, or world need proper tools to provide fast and accurate information, if necessary, in other languages.

We were involved in consulting opportunities at an extensive local school system with the management and supervisory team of the service departments. It was a union organization, and the director was familiar with our leadership development program from a previous company we had worked with. As a part of the consulting program, we would perform a de-hassle process for thirty key individuals. The representation included managers, supervisors, and leads, including union members. Throughout a few sessions, we were able to get over one hundred issues identified. Once the list was created, we began to force rank the issues into buckets based on priority and responsibility. The group was skeptical of getting through the process and for every voice to be heard; however, once completed, the group became closer and realized how certain decisions would not be in the best interest of the entire school district. We were able to make critical changes that provided excellent outcomes and solidified the group to work as a team.

As we move through creating the path of organizational change, we are beginning to see the importance of identifying the rowers within our organizations. Their positive influence on an organization's employees, clients, and finances has proven invaluable. Skills are essential, but in the end, the rower's personality and positive leadership skills develop consistent performance.

Epilogue

What lies behind us and what lies before us are tiny
matters compared to what lies within us.
—Oliver Wendell Holmes

It seems logical that when we manage or lead organizations, we should look for mistakes, areas of low production, or weaknesses within operations to improve production. Over the past twenty years or so, organizations have focused on culture as an opportunity to enhance the work environment. However, when the going gets rough and profits fall, panic sets in, and we go back to looking for what we did wrong instead of what we're doing right. As we have reviewed in the early chapters, our brains, based on the need to survive, focus first on the negative. And yet all the research indicates that focusing on what people do right, acknowledging and mirroring their success to other areas of the organization, increases productivity, creates a positive culture, decreases turnover, and increases profits.

The key is developing a team capable of providing consistently above-average services. Our research of more than thirty years and documented studies we have provided in this book point to a particular personality combination that can always offer above-average services. We refer to them as rowers. High-energy. Intrinsically motivated. Increased emotional intelligence. The right amount of empathy. Being proactive. These are some personality traits they possess.

We also provided the science and social learning behind increasing the productivity of the entire team, including the sitters, by focusing on and acknowledging the rowers' efforts. Finally, we introduced the driller as the source of most organizational issues. We identified drillers as ego-driven, wanting all attention to focus on their needs and desires, and identifying the error that managers consistently make in thinking they can change drillers into sitters or even rowers. Published data has proven that focusing attention on the drillers decreases productivity. Sitters become drillers through social learning; rowers become frustrated and leave.

The rower, sitter, and driller concepts provide a basis for leaders and managers to understand the composition of their teams and the rowers' value in the organization's overall success.

However, understanding the concept of rowers, sitters, and drillers is just the beginning. Recognizing and hiring people who can row and eliminate the risk of hiring drillers becomes the next challenge. In the parable about the three students and mastering how to row the boat, it became apparent who was the rower, sitter, and driller. During the hiring process, it can be challenging to identify potential drillers. The information we receive through interviews to make decisions is based on biases we have formed over the years we have lived and worked. We want to make the right decision, but we are working with information that could be incorrect.

In most cases, we go with the obvious or what we believe to be noticeable. After reading this book, do you believe that taking a chance is the best option? We created the Positive Assessment Tool^{sm} to remove our biases and provide a scientific hiring process. Assessments are not designed to find the best person for the position but to ensure we don't risk hiring the wrong person. No matter how good your interview process is, working without an assessment can be a costly mistake.

When working with most organizations and introducing the concept of rowers, sitters, and drillers, they quickly grasp it. Some even identify each of the three categories within their teams. We know who the energizers are and who the drillers are. We hope this book has created an urgency to identify and reward the rowers and deal effectively with the drillers.

Afterword

Find out who you are, and do it on purpose.
—Dolly Parton

P aul Fayad dedicated the last thirty years to studying personality and behaviors in the work environment. The effort has always been to provide a positive environment leading to higher quality and greater efficiencies in our services. When he met Dr. Chak Fu Lam, they recognized the opportunity to work as a team to accomplish our goal. The creation of Positive Leader, LLC, was the result of their collaboration. They realized that when we merge academics with business, we can uncover results and adjust quickly. Having the opportunity to oversee a national service company for over twenty years became a perfect testing platform for us to measure our results, adjust, and provide living proof that positive leadership was creating the positive results we expected. But we didn't stop there. The more awards we won and recognition we received, the more other organizations became interested in the process outlined in this book. It became a part of the Positive Leader mission to share what we discovered in our research to help other organizations understand the influence individuals had on the quality, quantity, and culture of organizations.

Key results of this period include:

- Focusing on what our staff did right was more important than pointing out what they did wrong.
- Providing praise and gratitude in public and correction in private, increasing awareness to other departments, and producing greater confidence in our staff.
- Using gain framing in performance feedback created a learning environment instead of a perceived punishment.
- Requesting feedback from the staff stimulated creativity.

As we continued implementing Positive Leader throughout our facilities, we noticed what would become the critical component of true success in all our locations. Positive results in some locations and not in others triggered the need to review which behaviors our managers brought to each site. Tying their behaviors to what were their inherent personalities created the need for an accurate tool. With the help of data and many years of results and comparisons to other results, we finalized the Positive Assessment Tool (PAT^{sm}). Although the assessment was a personality assessment tool, we chose the name PAT^{sm} as an all-inclusive measurement of what we found to be important in delivering successful leadership results.

Key results of this period include:

- The creation of the first PAT^{sm}.
- Tying the results to our successful managers.
- Establishing proper hiring processes around the PAT^{sm}.

But explaining the details of the research and the measurements of the assessment's results became lengthy and challenging to explain. The result was the decision to create the rower, sitter, and driller concept.

Key results of this period include:

- Rowers were the forever energizers who always wanted to row.
- The sitters were always willing to watch, waiting to decide their course of action, sometimes rowing and drilling, depending on the environment.
- Drillers were always looking for a way to drill, focusing on themselves and how they were affected, not knowing or caring about the team, the organization, or the outcome of their drilling.
- Skill or behavior wasn't necessarily the issue since people could be trained if they had a desire to learn.

We began to see which team members, especially our managers, were rowing, sitting, or drilling. The focus on success in the business world is predicated on results. As we see, time and time again, the results are affected by relationships and the culture within organizations. Drillers reduce morale and create disruption. They do not support change and look to divide and conquer. Through our research on inherent personalities, we knew they would not change; however, if they were removed, how could we be sure to replace them with rowers or at least sitters? The PAT^{sm} became even more critical. As noted above, the results were incredible, provided by the awards we received and our company's tremendous growth.

Key results of this period include:

- Developing the R+S+D/ABC skills matrix.
- Focus on hiring for talent (successful relationship personalities), not skill.
- Understanding the negative effects highly skilled drillers have on organizational culture.
- Focusing on rowers' skill development produced better outcomes than efforts to correct drillers.

Dr. Lam received his PhD in organizational behavior, providing more research to our ongoing learning. He has also created graduate-level coursework at universities on Positive Leader, which we have both had the privilege to lecture on and speak about over the past fifteen years. We both continue to consult with organizations throughout the world.

We focused many years on the effects of personalities and behaviors in business. We were primarily using the assessment as a recruiting tool. We began to see that the assessment could be used for relationship, team, and leadership development.

Key results of this period include:

- Modified the results to indicate High, Average, and Monitor.
- Modified the summary to provide more explicit detail for the new assessment.
- We created leadership development workshops around the individual's and the team's PAT^{sm} results and the rower, sitter, and driller concept in leading.

As fate would have it, my eldest son, Andrew, was following an organization called the DV Institute of Higher Learning, headed by a modern-day scholar and philosopher, Dhyan Vimal. In 2020, with the first wave of COVID restricting travel and locking us in our homes, it was the perfect opportunity to do more research and expand my reading. The institute provided many books and eventually established Zoom classes with Vimal. Then the opportunity to meet Vimal in person occurred in the spring of 2022. Our discussion, in private, involved many topics, but one became an ongoing discussion: rowers, sitters, and drillers, as well as the PAT^{sm}.

We began with a review of the staff of the DV Institute. Over the following months, after many adjustments and data reviews, the Positive Leader team was able to finalize the PAT^{sm} into an accurate leadership and relationship development tool.

Key results of this period include:

- The PAT^{sm} was finalized to indicate the four levels:
  » high

- » moderate
- » minimal
- » monitor
- We developed a newer and more detailed summary format.

As we analyzed the new data, we began to see patterns that were not obvious in the recruiting assessment analysis. When used for recruiting, we established specific data points and percentages to determine the best candidates for the organizations we were working with. Accumulating assessment results and analyzing the data in the new format provided us with a unique opportunity.

Key results of this period include:

- The percent of high awareness on average for all traits: 15.5 percent.
- The percent of monitor awareness on average for all traits: 14 percent.
- Moderate and minimal awareness made up the remaining: 70.5 percent.
- Slightly more moderate by less than 2 percent.
- Most individuals, in the business assessments and the individual assessments, averaged in the moderate awareness level slightly above the minimal awareness level.

The interesting part came from analyzing the data in relation to the rower, sitter, and driller concepts. Was there a correlation between assessment results and predetermining from the data if they were rowers, sitters, or drillers? The answer was turning out to be more complicated; in business, we need the best of the best, and we don't have the luxury of spending a lot of time training everyone, especially if the training won't produce the desired results due to inherent and immovable individual personality traits. It isn't always easy to leave everyone behind in our personal lives, although sometimes it is advisable. This is where the collaboration with Vimal created the answer. Through his established programs, we were able to define the rower, sitter, and driller. Once individuals receive their PAT^{sm} and the analysis, the resulting process can provide the individual with the choice to row, sit, or drill.

Key results of this period include:

- Factors that determine a rower:
  - » Key personality traits in the right combinations at high levels:
    - □ emotional intelligence, empathy, proactiveness, change mindset, intrinsic learning, growth mindset, communication style, participation, and focus on success.
  - » They accept their results as an opportunity to gain knowledge of their potential behaviors. Action taken.
  - » Willingness to use the ABC as a tool, respecting the response from others as a witness to their behavior, and adjusting accordingly.
  - » Create a path of change with enthusiasm and collaboration.
  - » Supportive to all, nonjudgmental.

- Factors that determine a sitter:
  - » A mixture of the personalities mentioned as a rower, more moderate levels.
  - » Accepting their results as an opportunity to gain knowledge into their potential behaviors. Action delayed, frozen.
  - » Difficulty in using the ABC as a tool, respecting the response from others as a witness to their behavior, and adjusting accordingly.
  - » Difficulty in establishing a path of change.
  - » Difficulty in supporting others. Looking for support.

- Factors that determine a driller:
  - » Lacking the personality traits mentioned as a rower, minimal or monitor levels.
  - » Minimal or unacceptance of their results, especially those at a monitor level.
  - » Difficulty using the ABC as a tool; ego-driven behavior causes them not to notice how others react to their presence. Blaming others for not understanding their behavior.
  - » Difficulty in establishing a path of change.
  - » Unsupportive, judgmental.

Suddenly, the realization was setting in that rowers were a tiny percentage of the population based on the data. Of course, drillers are also a small percentage of the population. The results indicated the majority were sitters.

The outcome of the PAT^sm allows individuals to see their true nature. Their resulting behavior will enable them to be a rower, sitter, or realize they could be a driller. The difficulty in changing who we are is still an issue.

If we accept an opportunity to learn and pause to watch the results through relationships with others, we all can hit the reset button and recreate ourselves. We can only present the opportunity and the path.

The decision to positively influence life is still up to the individual. The essential realization is that good humans look beyond themselves, using their relationships with others as an opportunity to grow and develop in business and their personal lives.

We hope you will jump into the boat, grab the oars, and row.

APPENDIX

The Positive Assessment Tool^{sm} Reviewed

Through our studies of behaviors and personalities, we can see how these voices or expressions can take root in our being, producing behaviors that can inhibit the realization of our true selves. We created the Positivity Assessment Tool (PAT^{sm}) with the intent to provide organizations with a tool to help them with the opportunity to see potential employees' inherent personalities and corresponding behaviors. Throughout its existence, it became a training tool to help develop leaders into rowers.

For some individuals, it can acknowledge who they are, providing peace within them. For others, it can acknowledge their frustration and disappointment from trying to be someone they are not. In other words, certain personalities lead to certain behaviors. We believe that, as an example, apathy can lead to depression, which can be caused by behaviors that are forced or not in line with our personalities. When I review the PAT^{sm} with individuals, and they realize and accept that their inherent personalities influence certain behaviors and outcomes, they can begin to set a new realistic course. Instead of frustration compared to others, they realize their path will involve certain adjustments, more energy, and a keen awareness that producing desired outcomes will not come naturally. They can move from sitting to rowing.

We also measure fixed mindsets with questions indicating if the individual has a fixed or a growth mindset. This helps those with a fixed mindset realize that compared to others with a growth mindset they will have to be more persistent in the learning process. Individuals with high awareness of empathy, compassion, praise, and instilling meaning can fall into the habit of providing everything for everyone, overextending themselves and believing they can make others happy. This unhealthy, one-sided relationship can lead to self-destruction. It can create a dependency of the other on them. One becomes frustrated, and the other lazy.

What Is a PAT^{sm}?

The PAT^{sm} is a standardized measure of personalities and behaviors. It is designed to help individuals better identify and understand their strengths and areas for improvement. This aids in personal development and the development of relationships. The assessment consists of 148 items, measuring personality traits that research has shown are valid predictors of organizational culture, performance at work, and personal relationship-building in life. PAT^{sm} meets the United States Equal Employment Opportunity Commission (EEOC) compliance requirements.

What Does PAT^{sm} Measure?

The PAT^{sm} produces six key indexes:

- Positive Leader Personality Index
- Positive Leader Change Mindset Index
- Positive Leader Service Mindset Index
- Positive Leader Learning Styles and Capacity
- Positive Leader Communication Styles
- Positive Leader Relationship Behavioral Index

Assessment Results Document

This document is designed to explain your results and what you can do to create a deeper awareness of those results. Although extensive research on personalities has shown that only minimal change can occur, understanding our personalities allows us to witness our behaviors because of our personalities. Accepting our personalities is the beginning of consciousness and provides a window into our actions that we may not have the opportunity to see without assessments. Therefore, be careful not to interpret minimally or monitor as a negative result; it isn't about getting all high levels, which may not necessarily be good. The point is not to determine your success, worth, or value from this assessment. The point is to learn and discover who you are and accept who you are, which is the strength and purpose of this assessment. This self-discovery can lead to us improving our behavior and focusing on how we affect those around us. Positively using this awareness means we do not use the information as a means of controlling or shaming others, as well as not glorifying ourselves. This is the concept of rowers, sitters, and drillers.

Rowers accept their resulting levels, high or low. They do not use their highs to intimidate others, and they celebrate the highs of others. They seek to understand their weaknesses and modify their behaviors to neutralize their personalities. They constantly seek self-improvement while understanding the other in the relationship.

Drillers are the opposite of rowers. They use their areas of highs as weapons to control or shame others. They attack others with high levels to lower the other so they do not have to own up to their behavior. Their relationship focus is selfish, not allowing the other to exist.

Sitters are in the middle. They can become content with their levels, whether high or low. They desire anonymity, seeking to blend into life without effort. At times they may row if the desire is high enough, and at times they may drill if persuaded by other drillers. They tend to be content with moving through life by the influence of others rowing or drilling.

We hope you will receive this information as an opportunity to open the window of self-awareness. The opportunity to use this information to create a consciousness that provides healthier decisions, healthier relationships, and healthy life.

The following are the twenty-three traits we identify through the assessment. Multiple questions for each trait provide us with accurate results.

Personality Index

The seven traits measured are directly related to the established research that these traits are inherent. Throughout an individual's life, they do not change significantly. Studies indicate that the maximum change of personalities measured is less than 7 percent. Understanding our personalities provides us with the opportunity for self-discovery. As you review this section, focus on the results as an opportunity to become conscious of why you may react to certain situations the same way repeatedly. No matter what the results show, based on your answers to the assessment, focus on awareness. Knowing yourself leads to self-improvement.

Although personalities are mostly unchangeable, behavior can be modified because of the personality. Behavior modification takes time and energy. Consider the person who is an introvert and who must speak in front of a large group of people. They can rise to the occasion, but it takes much more energy than an extrovert. The introvert must be completely prepared and practice the lecture repeatedly to become comfortable. They will be nervous, uncomfortable, and looking forward to the end of the lecture. After the lecture, they may be exhausted and need to relax alone. The extrovert is the opposite. They prepare but are not nervous. During the lecture, they are excited and sometimes even animated. After the lecture, they are energized and will stay to talk to individuals. Introverts can rise to the occasion and perform when necessary, but they will always be an introvert.

Each trait will provide ways to modify their behavior and always be aware of how they will default in each situation due to their inherent personality.

1. Agreeableness

Agreeableness is a personality trait that describes individuals who place others' needs before themselves. It is one of the big-five personality traits. They are empathic and find pleasure in helping others who need help.

Agreeableness reflects the individual's tendency to develop and maintain prosocial relationships. Individuals high in this trait are more trustworthy, straightforward, generous, compliant, modest, and tender-minded.

2. Conscientiousness

Conscientiousness is the personality trait that describes an individual as being careful and diligent when dealing with others. They are individuals who desire to do a task well and take their obligations to others seriously. Conscientious people are organized, efficient, self-disciplined, and act dutifully. Their behavior is planned to aim for achievement in all they do. They are hardworking and reliable. Conscientiousness is one of the big-five personality traits.

3. Perspective-Taking

Perspective-taking is the personality trait that describes an individual as having the ability to look beyond their point of view to see how another may think or feel about a situation or an idea. It is understanding an alternate point of view and perceiving a situation from another individual's senses. Perspective-taking is identified in two dimensions: perceptual and conceptual. The first dimension, perceptual perspective-taking, is a person's ability to understand others' experiences through their senses, such as visually or auditorily. Most research on perceptual perspective-taking focuses on the visual or the ability an individual has to understand the way others see things in a physical space. Conceptual perspective-taking is an individual's ability to comprehend and take on the viewpoint of others' psychological experiences, such as their thoughts, attitudes, and feelings.

4. Empathy

Empathy is the personality trait that defines an individual's ability to sense other people's emotions and imagine what someone else might be thinking or feeling. It is often described as mirroring or understanding another's emotion. Empathy can be divided into three types.

Cognitive empathy is knowing what another person feels and might be thinking. The understanding is limited to an awareness but not necessarily a desire to act.

Emotional empathy can take a physical form when we physically feel emotions for what someone else is experiencing. We connect emotionally with others by looking at ourselves and how their issues would affect us similarly.

Compassionate empathy is the culmination of understanding and feeling a person's issues and choosing to act to help them.

5. Emotional Intelligence

First Coined in 1990 by researchers John Mayer and Peter Salovey, emotional intelligence is the personality trait that is an individual's ability to understand and manage your own emotions, as well as recognize and influence the emotions of those around you. This includes emotions such as accepting criticism and responsibility, moving on after a mistake, being able to say no, sharing your feelings with others, and solving problems in a way that works for everyone involved. Most experts have established five elements of emotional intelligence. Self-awareness, or recognizing and understanding your emotions, is what you are feeling and why and appreciating how they affect those around you. It is self-regulation of your emotions, controlling your highs and lows. It is the motivation of self and others, empathy toward others and their experiences, and developed social skills, which is the ability to interact with others, keeping in mind all the above.

6. Modesty

Modesty is defined as having or showing a moderate or humble estimate of one's merits, importance, etc., free from vanity, egotism, boastfulness, or great pretensions. Modesty is linked with critical human values, such as simplicity, humility, and temperance. It is the opposite of vanity and conceit, two-character traits that have gained a lot of ground in our current world. A modest person neither needs nor wants to go out boasting about something.

7. Proactive Mindset

A *proactive mindset* is a tendency to recognize opportunities, take the initiative and action, and persevere until a meaningful change occurs. Proactive people always look ahead at future activities, projects, and events and anticipate needs, problems, and possible outcomes.

Change Mindset Index

The Change Mindset Index measures an individual's willingness to accept change. It indicates levels of leading, supporting, analyzing, and avoiding change. Some individuals are more open to change, whereas others prefer the status quo. Change mindsets can be divided into the following categories:

- Change champion: individuals with high levels often lead the change.
- Change supporter: individuals with moderate levels may not lead change but support change.
- Change analyst: individuals with minimal levels tend to analyze change, even challenging the change, and may or may not support the change.
- Change avoider: individuals who need to monitor their awareness of change often avoid change.

Service Mindset Index

A service mindset measures the extent to which an individual is devoted to serving others. Research has shown that an individual's desire to meet the needs of others and the amount of effort the individual puts forth is positively associated with a range of favorable outcomes, such as higher relationship satisfaction and, at work, better team performance. It is essential to understand that we provide this index as an additional measurement of an individual's ability to form relationships with others, even those who may not be a part of their inner circle of friends. Ultimately, all our relationships are based on how we treat each other. *Character* is how we treat those who can do nothing for us.

Learning Style and Capacity

The following traits are an individual's desire to learn, styles or factors of learning, and whether they feel they can increase their learning capacity. The two traits, intrinsic and extrinsic, provide the individual with a measurement of what factors motivate their learning. The theory of intelligence determines whether they feel intelligence can be increased through the learning process. The learning value results indicate the motivating factors influencing the individual to learn. Studies have found that learning throughout our lives improves our self-esteem and can increase life satisfaction, optimism, and belief in our abilities. It can even help those who suffer from depression and anxiety. The question regarding the capacity to learn allows the individual to see that learning can help with growth and provide an opportunity for the individual to see a brighter future potentially.

Communication Style

The following traits, candidness, and conflict management, are reviewed to measure an individual's communication style. The results indicate an individual's ability to provide feedback in a direct yet safe method and resolve conflicts while maintaining a positive relationship.

Relationship Development Index

The Relationship Development Index provides an assessment of an individual's relationship behaviors. Individuals with high awareness in this area understand the importance of maintaining positive relationships with everyone. Positive relationships have been linked to multiple health improvements. Healthy relationships lower the production of cortisol, the stress hormone associated with heart disease. Research has also shown that individuals in healthy relationships have a greater sense of purpose through a sense of well-being. This section reviews nine traits determining an individual's ability to form positive relationships with others.

1. Gratitude

Gratitude is the quality of being thankful, readiness to show appreciation for and to return the kindness, and thankfulness to others. It is a conscious, joyous emotion that an individual expresses when feeling thankful for something, whether tangible or intangible. It's a practice that requires acknowledgment of someone else's gesture toward us or to yourself when things are going well in your life.

2. Compassion

Compassion is the ability to understand others' pain and the desire to mitigate that pain somehow. Empathy is feeling another person's pain, whereas compassion is sympathetic consciousness and the willingness to take action to relieve the suffering of others. Research has shown that when we feel compassion, our heart rate slows down, and we secrete oxytocin, also known as the bonding hormone, which lights up regions of our brain linked to empathy, caregiving, and feelings of pleasure, resulting in our wanting to approach and care for other people.

3. Praise

Praise is expressing admiration or approval of the achievements or characteristics of a person or actions of an event. There are three main types of praise. The first is personal praise specific to an individual. The second is effort-based praise, such as work accomplished by an individual or a team. And the third is behavior-specific praise based on individuals exhibiting specific positive behavior.

4. Meaning

Meaning is providing purpose and meaning for others through positive recognition. It is acknowledging others' contributions and creating significance for what others do by identifying and providing direct feedback.

5. Vision

Vision provides a vivid mental image of the future based on goals and aspirations. Vision provides direction and timely reviews of our life. It helps to make our goals and purpose become a reality. It gives us an understanding of ourselves and where we want to be. Through the knowledge of our vision, we can understand our purpose, and life can become less complicated and more meaningful.

6. Participation

Participation indicates the ability to include others in performance goal setting, making decisions, and creating a vision.

7. Intimidation

Intimidation is using words, actions, or implied threats to intimidate and threaten others to act. Intimidation can cause others to be fearful and apprehensive about responding or offering feedback.

8. Focus on Success

Focus on success means focusing on what others do right instead of focusing on errors and mistakes and trying to correct them.

9. Task Focused

These individuals focus on getting a job done without worrying about the personal development or satisfaction of the team. They are concentrated on assigning tasks, monitoring progress, and using standard procedures.

Bibliography

Allen, Summer. "Why Is Gratitude So Hard for Some People?" *Greater Good Magazine*. May 10, 2018.

Association for Psychological Science. "Narcissists Look Like Good Leaders—But They Aren't!" August 9, 2011. Accessed January 24, 2024. https://www.psychologicalscience.org/news/releases/narcissists-look-like-good-leadersbut-they-arent.html.

Atkinson, Charlie. "Neuroplasticity: Neural Networks in the Brain." *Short Communications* 8, no. 3 (March 25, 2021).

Bass, B. M. "The Future of Leadership in Learning Organizations." *Journal of Leadership Studies* 7, 3 (2000): 18–40.

Baumeister, R. F., Bratslavsky, E., Finkenauer, C., and Vohs, K. D. "Bad Is Stronger than Good." *Review of General Psychology* 5, 4 (2001): 323–70. https://doi .org/10.1037/1089-2680.5.4.323.

Bergs, Anthony. "5 Steps to Creating a Process-Centric Organization Without Losing Human Touch!" BPM Institute. Accessed January 24, 2024. https://www.bpminstitute. org/resources/articles/5-steps-creating-process-centric -organization-without-losing-human-touch-1.

Bleidorn, Wiebke, Schwaba, Ted, Zheng, Anqing, Hopwood, Christopher J., Sosa, Susana S., Roberts, Brent W., and Briley, D. A. "Personality Stability and Change: A Meta-Analysis of Longitudinal Studies." *Psychological Bulletin* 148, 7–8 (July-August 2022): 588-619. doi: 10.1037/bul0000365.

Bonnelle, Valerie, Manohar, Sanjay, Behrens, Tim, and Husain, Masud. "Individual Differences in Premotor Brain Systems Underlie Behavioral Apathy." *Cerebral Cortex* 26, 2 (February 2016): 807-819. doi: 10.1093/cercor/bhv247.

Bouchard Jr., Thomas J., and Loehlin, John C. "Genes, Evolution, and Personality." *Behavior Genetics* 31, no. 3 (June 26, 2001): 243–73.

Cherry, Kendra (2020). "What Is Negativity Bias?" Last modified November 13, 2023. Accessed January 24, 2024. https://www.verywellmind.com/negativebias-4589618.

Derler, Andrea, and Ray, Jennifer. "Why Change is so Hard—and How to Deal with It." NeuroLeadership Institute, December 12, 2019. Accessed January 24, 2024. https://

neuroleadership.com/your-brain-at-work/growth-mindset-deal
-with-change.

Doty, James R. "Scientific Literature Review Shows Health
Care Delivered with Kindness and Compassion Leads to
Faster Healing, Reduced Pain." Presentation at the Inaugural
Compassion and Healthcare Conference, Stanford University
School of Medicine. November 12, 2014. Accessed January 24,
2024. https://www.dignityhealth.org/about-us/press-center/
press-releases/scientific-literature-review-with-stanford.

Ericsson, K. A., Krampe, R. T., and Tesch-Römer, C. (1993).
"The Role of Deliberate Practice in the Acquisition of Expert
Performance." *Psychological Review* 100, 3 (1993): 363–
406. https://doi.org/10.1037/0033-295X.100.3.363.

Folkman, Joseph. "Your Inconsistency Is More Noticeable
Than You Think." *Forbes Magazine.* October 17, 2019.
Accessed January 24, 2024. https://www.forbes.com/sites/
joefolkman/2019/10/17/your-inconsistency-is-more-noticeable
-than-you-think/?sh=e3947643d507.

Gallup. *State of the American Manager: Analytics and Advice for
Leaders.* 2015.

Gallup. *State of the Global Workforce: 2022 Report.* Accessed
Jan. 24, 2024. https://www.cca-global.com/content/latest/
article/2023/05/state-of-the-global-workplace-2022-report-346/

Gladwell, Malcolm. *Outliers*. New York: Little, Brown and Company, 2011.

Goleman, Daniel. *Emotional Intelligence: Why It Can Matter More Than IQ*. New York: Random House, 2005.

Gurdjieff, G. I. *In Search of Being*. Boulder, Colo.: Shambhala Publications, Inc., 2021.

Humphrey, Albert. "Strength, Weaknesses, Opportunity, and Threats." Stanford Research Institute, 1960.

Kanter, Rosabeth Moss. "Ten Reasons People Resist Change." *Harvard Business Review*, September 25, 2012. Accessed January 24, 2024. https://hbr.org/2012/09/ten-reasons-people-resist-chang.

Ledgerwood, Alison, and Boydstun, Amber E. "Sticky Prospects: Loss Frames Are Cognitively Stickier Than Gain Frames." *Journal of Experimental Psychology General* 143, 1 (2014): 376-85. Advance online publication, March 25, 2013. doi: 10.1037/a0032310.

Lee, Yeunjae. "Dynamics of Symmetrical Communication Within Organizations: The Impacts of Channel Usage of CEO, Managers, and Peers." *International Journal of Business Communication* 59, 1 (2018): 3–21.

Lyubomirsky, Sonja. *The How of Happiness*. New York: Penguin Press, 2008.

Melita Prati, L., Douglas, C., Ferris, G. R., Ammeter, A. P., and Buckley, M. R. "Emotional Intelligence, Leadership Effectiveness, and Team Outcomes." *The International Journal of Organizational Analysis* 11, no. 1 (2003): 21–40. Accessed January 24, 2024. https://doi.org/10.1108/eb028961.

Mulqueen, Casey and Wolson, Natalie. "Bias in the Workplace: Using Neuroscience to Improve Training." *Training Industry*. November 4, 2015.

NeuroLeadership Institute. "5 Ways to Spark (or Destroy) Your Employees' Motivation." September 13, 2022. Accessed January 24, 2024. https://neuroleadership.fi/blog/5-ways-to-spark-or -destroy-your-employees-motivation-2/.

Nikos-Rose, Karen. "Scientists Say You Can Change Your Personality." *ScienceDaily*. (December 12, 2019). Retrieved January 23, 2024 from www.sciencedaily.com/ releases/2019/12/1912121659.htm.

Owens, B. P., Baker, W. E., Sumpter, D. M., and Cameron, K. S. "Relational Energy at Work: Implications for Job Engagement and Job Performance." *Journal of Applied Psychology* 101, 1 (2016): 35–49.

Romano, John. "Jon Cooper teaches. He motivates. He delegates. Mostly, he just wins." *Tampa Bay Times*, July 4, 2021.

Siegel, Daniel J. *Mindsight: The New Science of Personal Transformation*. New York: Bantam, 2010.

Sinek, Simon. *Leaders Eat Last: Why Some Teams Pull Together and Others Don't*. Google Books, 2014.

Spreitzer, Gretchen M., Lam, Chak Fu, and Quinn, Ryan W. "Human Energy in Organizations: Implications for POS From Six Interdisciplinary Streams." *The Oxford Handbook of Positive Organizational Scholarship*, edited by Kim S. Cameron and Gretchen M. Spreitzer, 156–167. New York: Oxford University Press, 2012.

Star Trek II: The Wrath of Khan, Paramount Pictures, June 4, 1982.

Suda. Tenth-century Byzantine encyclopedia dictionary, circa 950 CE.

Szcześniak, Malgorzata, Rodzeń, Wojciech, Malinowska, Angieszka, and Kroplewski, Zdzisiaw. "The Big Five Personality Traits and Gratitude: The Role of Emotional Intelligence." *Psychology Research and Behavior Management* 13 (November 11, 2020): 977–988. doi: 10.2147/PRBM.S268643.

TheSportster.com. "Top 15 Worst Locker Room Cancers in NFL History." January 7, 2015. Accessed January 24, 2024. https://www.thesportster.com/football/top-15-locker-room-cancers-in-nfl-history/.

Treadway, Michael, and Welsh, Jennifer. *Journal of Neuroscience.* May 1, 2012. Updated January 19, 2022, in LiveScience.

Vimal, Dhyan. Series of lectures, DV Institute for Higher Learning, 2023.

Waugh, Christian, Fredrickson, Barbara, and Taylor, Stephan. "Adapting to Life's Slings and Arrows: Individual Differences in Resilience When Recovering from an Anticipated Threat." *Journal of Research in Personality* 42 (2008): 1031-1046. 10.1016/j.jrp.2008.02.005.

Wharton Executive Education. "Five Minutes to Great Meetings: Start with the 'Power Lead.'" March 2018. Accessed January 24, 2024. https://executiveeducation.wharton.upenn.edu/thought-leadership/wharton-at-work/2018/03/five-minutes-to-great-meetings/.

Acknowledgments

We would like to acknowledge the following people, who have been influential in our lives and in our constant search for knowledge:

- Dhyan Vimal, master, guru, scholar, DV Institute, president of Friends to Mankind.
- Sang Kyu Shim, grandmaster of United Tae Kwon Do, president of the World Martial Arts Association, scholar. Deceased.
- George Makdisi, scholar, professor of Arabic and Islamic studies, and director of the Center for Medieval Studies: Islam, Byzantium, and Latin West, University of Pennsylvania. Deceased.

Additionally, we would like to sincerely thank the following people: My wife, Debra, who has had to listen to my nonstop discussion on organizational behavior; positive leadership; and rowers, sitters, and drillers for the better part of twenty-five years. My cousin Jeanne Makdisi helped edit and kept me motivated through questions and comments from her remote home in the Poconos.

My son Andrew—my business partner, study partner, and who without having introduced me to Dr. Chak Fu Lam, the DV Institute, and Master Dhyan Vimal, this book may never have happened.

Finally, to Chak Fu Lam—professor, "adopted son," and friend. Thank you for your guidance in cocreating Positive Leader, LLC; the PAT^{sm}; and the rowers, sitters, and drillers concept.

Additional Resources

- Positive Leader, LLC, Positive Assessment Tool (PAT^sm) as a hiring and training tool: https://positiveleader.com/.
- Positive Assessment Tool (PAT^sm) for individuals can be taken online at our website: https://positiveleader.com/.
- The DV Institute of Higher Learning: https://www.dhyanvimalinstitute.com/.

Through the institute, more information can be obtained on Dhyan Vimal's Six Rites of Creation, the ABC of Relationships, Living in Creation, Living a Self-Determined Life, and many more topics on personal development.

About the Authors

Paul Fayad was CEO of HHA Services, a large health-care organization, for twenty-two years. In 1997 Fayad established a hiring process based on personality and behaviors, and in 2000, he created Q-School, through which he personally taught all managers and executives the importance of positive leadership skills.

Under his leadership, HHA achieved numerous national awards for customer service and associate satisfaction and in 2004, HHA was given "Navigator Status" by the Michigan Quality Council in quality management initiatives as measured by Malcolm Baldridge criteria.

His focus on positive leadership led him to be the cofounder of Positive Leader and ELM Learning. Fayad has consulted with multiple organizations nationwide to establish leadership programs. He has lectured at universities and college business schools in the United States, Canada, and Hong Kong, and has been invited as a national speaker to more than twenty conferences.

Fayad, who holds an MSA in business with a focus on organizational behavior, has written numerous articles in trade journals and books and has written and produced over seventy industry training videos and digital modules on customer services and positive leadership.

He produced the documentary *Helambu: How One School Changed Everything*, which was the winner of the London Film Festival and finalist at the Banff and Vancouver film festivals.

He cofounded and is active with the East Side Youth Sports Foundation. He is dedicated to helping disadvantaged children in Detroit participate in sports and literacy programs. Fayad is active with the Tsering Fund in Nepal, providing young girls and orphans with education through scholarships. He is involved with Friends to Mankind and the Dhyan Vimal Institute, based in Canada and Malaysia, providing coursework in leadership and self-development. Fayad has worked with Habitat for Humanity, renovating and building homes in Detroit and internationally in Hungary.

Fayad studied martial arts for more than twenty years, and owned and operated martial arts studios in the Detroit metropolitan area. He is an avid high-altitude trekker worldwide, has played and coached amateur ice hockey for more than thirty years, and was named the 2014 Michigan Amateur Hockey Association Coach of the Year.

in ⊙ paulfayad

Chak Fu Lam cofounded Positive Leader with Fayad. Lam is an associate professor of management at City University of Hong Kong and in 2023 was a recipient of the Poets&Quants "40-Under-40 Best MBA Professors." Lam studies leadership, communication, self-determination, and well-being at work.

He has published research in premier management journals, such as *Academy of Management Annals*, *Academy of Management Perspective*, *Academy of Management Review*, *Journal of Applied Psychology*, *Journal of Management*, *Journal of Organizational Behavior*, *Organizational Behavior and Human Decision Processes*, and *Personnel Psychology*.

Lam is an associate editor for the *Academy of Management Review*, and serves on the editorial boards of *Journal of Applied Psychology*, *Journal of Organizational Behavior*, and *Management and Organization Review*. In 2021 he was one of five reviewers to be awarded the title of best editorial reviewer for his service to the *Journal of Applied Psychology*. He received his BA in psychology and economics from Middlebury College in Vermont and a doctorate in management and organization from the University of Michigan.

in chakfu

chak.fu

Positive Leader, LLC

At Positive Leader, we believe that a positive leadership focus coupled with emotional intelligence is the cornerstone of success, and we are committed to guiding individuals and companies toward achieving their full potential.

positiveleader.com

ELM Learning, Inc

At ELM, we combine the best practices in adult learning theory with visually captivating content, and we craft training that transcends the ordinary. Our commitment lies in delivering superior learning experiences that endure, fostering continuous growth and mastery.

elmlearning.com